Bake You

(Everything You Need to Know to Open Your Bakery)

Written by: Tiffany Nicole Holley

Preface: Everything you need to know to open your bakery

For God hath not given us the spirit of fear; but of power, and of love, and of a sound mind.

(KJV 2 Timothy 1:7)

I (your name)_____ declare victory over my life, I speak financial freedom over my life, I speak a prosperous business for the days and years to come. This is my year because I declare it will be in the name of Jesus, Amen.

Before you start reading this book, I ask that you read it with an open heart and open mind. I ask that you read this book with an expectancy to learn and gain knowledge, wisdom, and some business facts that you did not know before. I am an educator, and it does my heart good to know that my students have learned. If you read this book and follow my steps, this book can be your roadmap to starting or revamping your business. Remember, nothing worth having comes easy, so you are going to have to do some work, but I promise you that with an open heart and mind, nothing is impossible. So, if you are ready, let us begin with prayer.

Dear Lord, I ask that you bless the person that is reading this book. I ask that you manifest all their hearts desires and help them to live a life that only they could dream of. I ask that you grant them the same grace and mercy that you have granted me so many times in my life. I ask that you open the readers' hearts and minds so that they will receive knowledge and a blessing by reading this book. In Jesus' name, Amen.

Chapters

Chapter 1: Annie's 7UP Pound Cake (Preparing You to Become a Business Owner)

Chapter 2: Tippy's Sugar Cookie (Establishing Your Business)

Chapter 3: Strawberry Delight (Building Your Faith)

Chapter 4: Georgia Peach (Boosting Your Positivity)

Chapter 5: Choc Me Baby (How Bad Do You Want Your Business to Succeed?)

Chapter 6: Tippy's Red Velvet

Chapter 7: Granny's Apple Pie (The Reason Why You Love to Bake)

Chapter 8: Lemon Berry (The Beauty of Being an Entrepreneur)

Chapter 9: Birthday Bash (Getting Excited About Your Business)

Chapter 10: Chocolate Espresso (Time to Add Some Heat and Pressure)

Chapter 11: Tippy's Chocolate Chip Cookies (Learning How to Self-Motivate)

Chapter 12: Raspberry Drizzle (Prepping and Planning for the Opening of Your Bakery)

I am Super Duper excited that you took the time and money to buy my little--well, not so little--book! I hope that this book is everything to you like it is to me! I hope that this book will make you laugh, frown, gasp for air, and laugh again! I will tell you how I got over having to close my bakery, go through a divorce, and move across the state, and how I finally found true love and happiness, opened another successful bakery, and started living the life I had always dreamed of! But trust me, this ride was not easy. As a matter of fact it was like the scariest rollercoaster you have ever ridden. So, buckle up, hold on tight, and let the ride begin!!!

I would first like to thank my husband, Kevin. When I say you are AWESOME, I mean that with every breath in me, and I am so thankful that you chose me as your life partner. Your patience is AMAZING, and I just want to say that since marrying you, you make me want to be a better human being. To my best friend--whom I wish was still the little girl with the big ole ponytail and bright eyes following me around like a shadow--, Ania, my daughter, my counselor and confidant: I am so proud of the young, talented lady you have become. I know you will be the best RN that the world has ever seen because you are so loving and caring. I hope to one day be your patient! To my son Javaunte Jr, who teaches me the many chapters of patience and tough love, I am so proud to call you my son. You are the definition of a hustler (because you hustle me all the time lol). I love your mannerisms, and you are such a gentleman. I am blessed and fortunate that God gave me the title of being your mother. You two are smart, intelligent, funny, loving, spoiled and many other things, and I would not trade you for anything in the world. To my parents, who after 49 years of marriage are still funny and lovable, I really appreciate every moment I get to spend with the two of you, and I am thankful that God gave me you two as my parents who just so happen to love cooking. Finally, to my aunts, Sherry Norfleet and Rosie-Marie Henderson, I love you two ladies, you have always supported me in ALL my endeavors, and I know I have had a few lol. Sherry, you have the heart and soul of an angel. You are the aunt that I call to tell all about my day. Rosie you are the soul of an aunt who you call when you need to be uplifted and hear those words, "Baby, it's going to be alright." I am thankful to call both of you my aunts, and I love you two dearly! I would also like to give a shout out to all my friends who have motivated me throughout this journey of life. I do not take your friendship for granted, so if I call you my friend or sis, you are a gemstone in my life.

Chapter 1: Annie's 7UP Pound Cake (Preparing You to Become a Business Owner)

This chapter is titled *Pound Cake* because there is going to be some pounding, whipping, molding, and shaping you into the Super Bad Ass you were born to be. Let us begin by erasing the whole idea that we need to be PERFECT, and that our lives are supposed to be perfect... I am the most imperfect angel God has probably ever created lol. As a matter of fact, my imperfections are what makes me... ME! I would like to think and say that I have a heart of gold. Anyone who knows me can vouch that I truly love being around people (well, sometimes).

No, honestly, I am really a people pleaser so much so that I was once an educator. That is right, I was a Cosmetology Educator for eight years, and I loved every single moment of it! Teaching is in my DNA. As a matter of fact, the only reason why I am not an educator right now is because the school that I moved across state to teach at (we will get to that in a later chapter) filed for bankruptcy and closed... shattering my little teaching dreams. But that is ok, because if that would have never happened, I would have never moved back home to little ole Harlem, Georgia and found the love of my life!!

I love to make people laugh, smile, and feel good about themselves. I also have somewhat of a potty mouth, I probably could curse with the best of them. As a matter of fact, when I used to get mad or argue with someone, it was my mission to make them feel as short as me (5'3). But thanks to growing, and life lessons, and Kevin, I try not to be labeled as a sailor kid for my mouth... but every now and then, one or two of the not-so-good words come out.

In this life journey, you must understand that you are the captain of your own boat. What makes you happy is solely up to you. Once you figure that out, it is your responsibility to make yourself happy. You will stop putting so much power into other individuals, and you will start doing what makes YOU happy. Trust me, this is not an easy task. As a matter of fact, it took me over 40 years to figure this one out, but once I did, it was on and popping! I learned how to use the word NO without feeling guilty or bad, and it made my world a much better place. I know I too once wanted to be everything--and everybody--to everyone. But when you are giving too much of yourself to others, what do you have to give to yourself?

Have you been feeling tired lately or saying you need to go get a facial or try some new Fenty makeup to hide those dark circles under your eyes? Honey, I have the remedy for you! Learn to take a little time off for YOU. If you can, you need to commit at least one day out of the week to just you. If you want to sleep in until the sun is blaring through your blinds, do just that. If you want to lay on the sofa in your pajamas or t-shirt and leggings (like I do most of the time), and watch Netflix or old episodes of *Insecure* all day, then guess what? Do *that*! That is your prerogative.

To even take it up a notch, try leaving your cellphone on your nightstand, and just enjoy the day. You will be amazed at how long the day is when you do not have your phone in your hand. Meditate, ride your bike (stationary for me), go for a jog (walk for me), soak in your new bath salts you ordered from Etsy, and just enjoy YOU. If you do not feel like cooking for that day, order take out or go somewhere and enjoy a lunch or dinner all by yourself. We have to learn how to take time out for ourselves, because trust me, you don't want Mrs. Burnout to come knocking on your door. Sometimes your body may do some uncontrollable things like shut down or give you a stomach virus just so you have to stay home for a day or two. And I don't know about you, but I'd rather give my body the proper rest she needs. So quick recap, what are we going to start scheduling on our calendar for next week? A Me Day! If you are not able to devote a whole day, start with an hour or two. I promise you, you will thank me later!

So, back to learning the word NO... I am not saying to just shout the word out like a little two-year-old who has just learned how to say it. If there is truly something you will not have time to do, or if it will put you in a pickle, simply state, "I apologize, but I can't." Prime example: at my bakery, Tippy Cakes, customers--God bless their little souls--love to call and order a custom cake that is either to be picked up the next day, or even worse, the same day. Well, because I like to bake my cakes fresh instead of having them stacked in the freezer, that task is a little... impossible. In the beginning I used to try to please everyone. I would take that order and guess what? While that customer was peacefully sleeping, dreaming about picking up my sweet, moist cake for the next day, I would be working in the wee hours of the night, tired and exhausted with a husband and kids wondering, "Where is mommy and why is she not home with our dinner???"

So, to make sure my family was fed at a decent time (and that I was not overly exhausted before the next day), I kindly started using the word NO. If you are a baker like myself, I am sure you get this request ALL OF THE TIME. I can even put it in a nice sentence for you: "I apologize, but we will not be able to have a cake available for pick up on such short notice." Just smile and tell them you require at least a four-day notice, and next time, hopefully they will remember to order in advance. If not, hey! There's always Walmart or Publix who have delicious cakes waiting in the freezer for purchase.

You need to learn when your plate is full. I can laugh and say this one because I am always doing two to three things at a time. As a matter of fact, while writing this book, I am also running a full-time bakery, an Etsy store where I sell homemade candy and sprinkles, and--as if that were not enough--I have found a new love for making stationary for my bakery needs such as: tags, cupcake picks, cake toppers, logos, stickers etc. So, when my days off come around (normally Sunday and Monday), I try to take one of those days to rest or sleep in a little. I like to kick my feet up on the sofa while working on my laptop or designing something with my silhouette cameo. Although my bakery is closed Sunday-Tuesday, that does not mean I get to be off those three days. Once you open your business, you will see that we truly do not get that many days off, especially when you're first starting a business.

There is always something that needs to be done, ordered, filled, and so on. But on my days off, I enjoy not being rushed and not leaving home unless it is an absolute must. When I learned to say, "No," or, "Sorry, I can't," and learned how to not overextend myself, life got a whole lot chiller! I mean, there are some days where I may have a little stress over a cake order or something of that nature, but I hardly ever stress over work anymore. Remember: you must learn to do only as much as you can bare and save the rest for a later date.

So, you want to bake, right? I mean, that is one of the reasons why you brought my book, yeah? So that I can tell you this magical saying to make all your baking dreams come true? LOL. Just kidding, I do not know any magical spells to make all of your bakery dreams come true, but what I *do* know is that hard work, dedication, determination, grit, resilience, and a few other fancy words is what has kept me in the marathon for this long. Oh yeah, and let us not forget about learning how to ignore that BIG WORD "NO," and how to grow some tough skin. There are going to be times where you want to cry like a baby. I mean throw yourself on the floor like a little baby and kick, scream, and cry your eyes out. And you know what? That is perfectly fine. Throw your temper tantrum and get your butt right back up and try again. Running a business is all about trying again and again. I still do not have this bakery thing figured out 100%, but I do what works for me, and you will learn to do what works for you. So, are you ready to bake this pound cake? This is where you will want to grab your highlighter or take notes. This is some good stuff!

I. Ask yourself the million-dollar question: Why do I want to start a business? (FYI, this can be any kind of business, not just a bakery!)

_____

_____

_____

_____

II. What does this business mean to me?

_____

_____

_____

_____

III. What would starting/opening a business help me achieve?

_____

_____

_____

IV. How do I plan to start/open this business?

_____

_____

_____

_____

V. Do I have a Business Plan? (No worries if you don't now, we will get into all of that later.)

_____

_____

_____

_____

VI. How will I fund this business? (E.g., Savings, Loans, Grants, Cash App, My Job, Part-time Job, Husband/Boyfriend, Wife/Girlfriend, Family & Friends etc.)

_____

_____

_____

_____

VII.   How will I tell everyone about my business?

_____
_____
_____
_____

VIII. Will my business be an actual brick-and-mortar building or online only?

_____
_____

IX.   Will I be a Sole Proprietor, LLC, S Corporation, etc.?

_____
_____

X.   Last but the most important of all questions, what is the name of my business?

_____
_____

Well, my friend, if you honestly took the time to answer the ten questions I presented to you, you have just done your BUSINESS PLAN!!! That was easier than you thought, right? I know just hearing the word "business plan" makes you cringe, but the good thing is, you can make it as casual and simple as the one you just completed. Now that you have that out of the way, you can later type up your business plan, put it in one of those fancy pocket folders with the sheet protectors or a cute binder, and save it for when you're trying to secure funds, or when you're on the floor throwing a temper tantrum, asking yourself, "Why did I want to start this business anyway?!" This will be a grand reminder of the why (and how) you will make it happen!

When I first started baking, I started right at home in my kitchen, and just like you, I brought every cake decorating magazine and every cake decorating tool. The cashiers at Michaels, JoAnn's, Hobby Lobby, A.C. Moore, and Walmart knew me by name. This was also before I discovered Amazon, so I would order from eBay and have to wait a month or so before the products I ordered from China arrived. Sometimes, I would even forget I had ordered something, but I would be just as excited and happy when it did finally arrive.

I had more rolling carts than I can count, and let us just say I had turned my dining room into a full-blown bakery. Lord, I would like to apologize to my ex-husband because all he wanted to do was come home from work without having to tiptoe over all my baking stuff. Well guess what? Now I have a bakery in my laundry room! I'm super-duper excited. I just got a She Shed delivered to my back yard so that I can have space for my 500 cake pans that I'm probably never going to use again. I will get around to donating them one day, but I must admit, I am a cake decorating, cake supply JUNKIE… there, I said it. I LOVE everything about baking & decorating. It is my therapy, it soothes me, it makes me happy. And that is why I decided to make this my job, my career. But let me tell you, it was not always peaches and cream.

Are you ready for a funny story? I mean a *really* funny story. Ok. Here you go. I am a self-taught baker, meaning I taught myself how to bake. I started off using cake box mix, then I learned how to add ingredients and make that same cake box mix taste like a homemade cake baked from scratch. I will give you some good recipes later, I promise! I believe it was my daughter Ania's 4th or 5th birthday, and I can remember she LOVE, LOVE, LOVED the Bratz dolls. Her room was hot pink with the Bratz border, her curtains were Bratz, her bedspread was Bratz, she had the Bratz DVDs, Bratz dolls galore… you get the picture, right? Well, I was super excited to be baking Ania's birthday cake for her birthday party at "Funs Ville." It was a party place that had go karts, kiddie rides, arcade games, etc. I had invited family, friends, and some of her friends from her school. I remember baking the cake, going to Walmart, and purchasing a Bratz Dolls cake kit to go on top of her cake. I wanted this cake to be special for her birthday party.

Fast forward to the birthday party. We get to there, and I proudly carry the cake inside. I sit it on the table we had reserved for her birthday party. She is so excited to see her friends from school, her grandparents and she is bursting with anticipation to go play the games and ride the kiddie rollercoasters. Her grandfather, who just so happens to be a retired Drill Sergeant from the Army, walks over, looks at the cake, and then he starts to walk around to other guest tables and look at their birthday cakes. He comes back to me with a straight face and says, "Tiffany, where is the manager or who is running this place?" I asked him why, and he says, "Because I want to know why everyone else that is having a birthday party here has cakes that look beautiful and my granddaughter's cake looks JACKED up." "He really said something else that I can't repeat in this book lol". If I could have turned pink, purple, and yellow, I am sure I did. Looking back at this, I can see why my ex and I are divorced today, because he looked me dead in my face earlier that day and told me the cake looked good.

I tried to laugh it off, and I told Ania's grandfather that *I* made the cake. He reached in his pocket, gave me $25, and told me to go to the nearest grocery store and to get his grandbaby a birthday cake. That should have been the day that ended my career. It should have crushed my dreams of wanting to bake ever, ever, ever again. But you know what I did? I took those twenty-five dollars, drove to Food Lion, and bought Ania a birthday cake, and that following Monday, I went to JoAnn's and signed up for my first Wilton Cake Decorating class.

There, I learned so much, I learned how to decorate a cake the correct way, how to use cake boards and dowels to separate my cakes. I learned how to make flowers and decorate with fondant. I took all four or five courses, and guess what? I even ended up being a Cake Decorating Instructor for Wilton--talk about turning a humiliating situation into a positive, powerful lesson. It has made me the coolest cake decorator that I am today!

Remember when I said you must grow some tough skin? That was one of those times. To be honest, I owe my cake decorating skills to Ania's grandfather, because if it wasn't for him being brutally harsh and honest, I would have thought that Lil Bratz cake was the bomb when, honestly, it looked like Ania (who was 4 or 5) made it.

I can't go without crediting my mother, Annie, for molding and shaping me not only into a pretty good baker, but a pretty good mother as well. I love her spirit. She is smart, funny, loving, youthful and welcoming. She always greets you with a smile no matter what, and I love the way her eyes light up when she is excited or when you mention a casino lol (she and my Aunt Marie love the casino). My mother and my father have to give you something to take home no matter what. They will not let you leave their house without a plate of food. They are so giving, and they love to cook big meals for the family.

A typical Sunday will consist of me and my siblings with our children and spouses at my parents' house, surrounded by laughter, jokes, love and, most importantly, eating. My mother is a very good cook. I'm not just saying that because she is my mother; she really is a great cook! She has her own catering business, and I have learned so much from her over the years about how to prep food, price catering events, handle nagging customers, prep and plan for events, and so much more.

When I first started my bakery and had catering jobs, I would sometimes call her to get her input and ask her how much she would charge for this or that, and sometimes she would call me and ask my input on certain catering jobs. My mother and Aunt Marie can really throw down in the kitchen. My mother's homemade macaroni and cheese casserole and roast beef are amazing. Her roast beef is so tender you can cut it with your fork, and my Aunt Marie's fried corn, fat back, and giblet gravy that go with my mother's dressing are so mouthwatering.

I cannot forget about my father either; he is a great cook also. He is known all over town for his BBQ and Hash, people from all over come to his house when he cooks his BBQ and Hash. I really wish he would open a BBQ pit because it is just that good (I might just have to make him to read this book so he finally will start that business). He loves to cook with peppers, and the family always jokes about his spicy dressing and spicy collard greens. He will have like three different types of peppers in them, but you can't stop eating them because they are so good. You just have to fix an ice-cold glass of tea to help soothe the hotness. My grandmother was like that--her dressing would be so spicy it would bring tears to your eyes, but you would keep coming back for more. I am so grateful to come from a family of cooks.

My 7Up Pound Cake recipe I use at the bakery is my mother's recipe, and customers cannot get enough of it. It is so moist and delicious, you can taste the lemon flavoring in the cake, it is one of my and my son's favorites. I also use her Red Velvet Cake recipe, but I add a few things to tweak it. Her Red Velvet Cakes are so velvety and moist, I could eat half a cake by myself. I only hope to one day be as a good as a baker as my mother and as good as a cook as my father.

Annie's 7 Up Pound Cake Recipe

3 cups sugar

3 sticks of butter (softened)

5 eggs

3 cups of Swans cake flour (must be Swans, per my mama)

¾ cup 7UP

2 teaspoons lemon flavoring

Cream sugar and butter together, add eggs one at a time. Next, add 2 teaspoons lemon flavoring, then ¾ cup of 7UP, then slowly add 3 cups of cake flour. Mix thoroughly. Preheat oven to 325 degrees Fahrenheit., grease or batter your pan, pour in contents, and bake for 1 hour and 15 minutes. Stick toothpick in cake to make sure it is completely done after the allocated time.

Chapter 2: Tippy's Sugar Cookie (Establishing Your Business)

The good thing about today versus seventeen years ago is SOCIAL MEDIA… I tell people all of the time, if it wasn't for Facebook, I would probably be working a nine-to-five job at a place I resented going to on a daily basis. When used correctly, social media can be your "meal ticket," or how the young girls say it today, "your bag," your money, your mula! Social media is the BEST thing they could have ever come up with for entrepreneurs such as yourself! We will NOT use Facebook, Instagram, or Twitter to look and see what your ex is doing or who is arguing or fighting with their baby mama or baby daddy. We have one mission: **Secure the bag**. In translation, MAKE MONEY! And sorry to tell you my friend, Drama is a freeloader that does not make you money.

The first thing you want to do is set up a separate page just for your business. I will be honest and frank with you. Yes, your kids are adorable, but customers are not on your page to see your family photos, your life history, and the newest outfit you brought from Tanger Outlets. Customers are visiting your business page for one purpose: to see what you have to offer and if they want to spend their money--their mula--with YOU.

So, let us make it as easy as possible for the consumer to spend their money with your business. Make sure to have clear, precise pictures of your product. Grab that highlighter again! I ordered a cute little ring light for my iPhone (they also have them for Androids!). You can search "Qiaya Selfie Ring Light for Phone" on Amazon or eBay. This gives your photos just enough lighting to make it look like it was taken professionally. The next thing I sometimes do is go to www.canva.com and upload my photos using some of their templates to make my photos look even more professional. They have hundreds of templates that you can use for free! Always make sure you watermark your photos so no one else can post your pictures and not give you the credit you so rightfully deserve (you can download an app on your phone to watermark or go to the "edit" section of your pictures on your phone).

If you are offering a product at a set price, you may want to list the price publicly so that consumers don't have to message you all day asking, "How much are your products?" (even though, chances are, they will still message you and ask). If you do not have a set price, or if it varies, you can always say, "starting at $__," to avoid those kinds of messages. And if someone asks how much your products are in the comments, please don't say, "Inbox me." Per research (and hearing some of my Facebook friends talk about it), customers *hate* when they want to purchase an item from you and you reply, "Inbox me." That can almost mess up the deal for you and cause you to lose that customer. People are more impatient these days than ever before. They want to know details about the product, the price, and how to purchase it with little to no interaction from the actual owner of the business. Just look at Amazon, eBay, Walmart.com, and MsHolley.com. You do not normally speak with the owner of those companies. That is the new way of shopping, and I seriously doubt it is going to change any time soon.

Another tip: Make sure your contact information is correct and up-to-date just in case someone wants to contact you. List your hours of operation. You can also use an after-hours message that will pop up when someone messages you after-hours or on a day that you are closed.

Make sure you interact with your potential consumers. Offer a discount or coupon if they are willing to share your business page with their friends and family. You can also do a free giveaway, but remember you are in the business of making money, not the business of giving it all away, so only do a giveaway if you are able to afford it! It can be something small and simple. People love FREE stuff!

I cannot speak for every state, but I can give you a few pointers for opening a business in the state of Georgia. The first thing you will want to do (grab your highlighter) is come up with a name for your business. Once you have a name, you will want to visit www.IRS.gov, and in the search bar, type in "EIN." Then, select "Apply for an Employer Identification Number (EIN) Online." Your EIN number will be like your business social security number. This will be helpful when you open a business checking account, or you try getting wholesale accounts because they will require you to provide your EIN number. You can also apply for a Dun & Bradstreet D-U-N-S® Number. This number is also used like a business social security number, and it can be used to help secure business funding. I am no business expert, but these are some things that were beneficial to me when I opened my bakery.

Lately, I have seen a lot of people on Facebook asking how to go about securing an LLC for their business. Let us dig a little deeper and find out what exactly an LLC is. According to The Preppy Family, an organization that helps small business owners advertise to their customers, "An LLC protects you and your personal assets—including your car, home, and bank accounts—from liability if your business is ever sued or incurs debts." Legalzoom.com says, "Unlike with a corporation, you aren't required to have a board of directors or shareholders with an LLC. You have more options in setting up your management structure." In short, LLCs provide entrepreneurs like us flexibility and security as we manage both our lives and businesses.

The other option is to become a sole proprietor. Unlike an LLC, sole proprietorship makes your business inseparable from your personal assets, meaning you will be responsible for all finances, loans, and liabilities associated with your business. While a sole proprietorship gives you greater control over your business, it does not offer you the same personal protections and securities that an LLC does.

I would say if you do not have an actual brick-and-mortar store front, you may not have to file for an LLC. But if you do decide to register your business for an LLC, you would go through your state. For example, in Georgia, you would go to Georgia.gov. Under the menu tab, you would click on "How-To Guides," or type, "applying for an LLC," in the search bar, and it should link you to the correct information. Once you have decided to apply for an LLC or register as a Sole Proprietor, you would go to the Department of Revenue and register your business. This is how you will ensure you are paying the correct taxes for your business. Trust me! You do not want to get a letter from the IRS stating you owe BIG MONEY for your business. Do it right the first time! Once you are under IRS watch it is hard to get off.

After you have registered your business, you will then search, "department of labor," on your state's website and register your business with the department of labor. This will assure you are paying the correct taxes. It will also allow you and your employees to apply for unemployment insurance should an emergency occur that prevents you from working for a period of time.

For example: during this COVID-19 pandemic, if you have a business and you registered with the Department of Labor, you will be able to apply for unemployment benefits for yourself. I do not know about you, but every little bit counts, *especially* in times like these.

As we go through the rest of the chapters, I will have a reference page that you will be able to go to for help with applying for the different business licenses and registering your business to the correct entities. I am super excited you are taking the big leap of faith of becoming an entrepreneur. I will give you all the knowledge that I have, and if there is something that I do not know, we can Google it together, or I can ask someone who may know a little more than I do. Either way, we will get through this so that you can own a legit, legal business!

Once, you have your EIN and you have registered with your state government, the Department of Revenue, and the Department of Labor, you will go to your local City Hall and apply for a business license in the city where your business will be located. This process is fairly easy and is usually $75 to $100 for the application. You may be required to have inspections by the Department of Agriculture, or the Health and Fire Department, and they will require their own application fee as well. Starting a new business can be pricey, but you want to ensure that everything is legit and legal.

I know that may have been a lot of information, but we will get through this together! Opening a business can seem overwhelming at times but it is also an exciting adventure. Picture the day you have your grand opening, and you are standing there in front of your family, friends, and new customers who all came to see and support YOU! It is a wonderful feeling, and it is your WHY behind opening a business in the first place.

Now that you are about to sign the lease on your brand-new business and you have filled all legal paperwork, let us talk a little bit about confidentiality and how to build your support system. If you are planning to hire someone to work in your bakery, you may want to have them sign a "Non-Disclosure" form and a "Non-Compete" form. I got both forms from Legal Zoom, but you can google different ones and make your own. Basically, a "Non-Disclosure" form protects your recipes and the way that you conduct business. If the person who signed this form were to share your recipes or try passing them off as their own, you would be entitled to sue that person. With the "Non-Compete" form, in the event your worker is fired or decides to quit, they cannot gain employment at another business that is similar to yours within however many miles you decide, or they are not allowed to start a business for themselves within however many miles you choose for a certain amount of time (it can be a few months, or up to 1-2 years). These contracts will ensure that the people you entrust with your business will not run off with your recipes and open a bakery across the street.

When looking to hire an assistant or build your team, one of the first things you will want to do is ask for professional references--not references from family and friends. Secondly, ask honest questions during the interview process like why they chose your business, what happened at their last place of employment and why are they no longer there, and where they see themselves in the next 2 to 5 years. Ask detailed questions like how they work under pressure. Lastly, make sure you have a list of all your demands and expectations upfront. For example: reporting to work on time, calling in before the shift begins if they are going to be late, how to properly greet the customers in-person and over the telephone, dress code if you have one, and so on. If you build a dependable team and state your demands from the beginning, you will be on your way to having a profitable business. Look at McDonald's for example, they could not operate without their team. With you being able to hire a team, it frees up some of your time and allows you to focus on other important things for your business, such as marketing.

If you are opening your business banking solely on your family and friends supporting you, sorry to give you the bad news, but you are not going to be in business for long! I could be wrong, but from having conversations with my friends that are business owners and my own personal experiences, we all say the same sentence: "Do not open a business expecting family and friends to support you." It's sad but true; you will find more strangers that will support your business than you will family. I cannot explain it. I used to get so frustrated and upset when I would post events or products and family wouldn't show up or buy. I have siblings, aunts, uncles, and cousins that have never stepped foot into my bakery. But I learned to focus on meeting as many strangers as I could, and that is what kept my business afloat. Focus on the customers who do support you and share your posts on Facebook and Instagram to their family and friends. In this day and age, social media allows you to meet strangers in your city, state, and places you will probably never visit who have the same interests as you and will support you.

Those are the people you want to know all about your business, and thanks to the wonderful USPS, FedEx, and other mail carriers, you can even ship your wonderful products all over the world. Opening a store on Etsy was an eye opener for me. I was amazed at how people would go on a website and order handmade products. All you have to do as a seller is package them up, print off the shipping label, and mail the package off. I loved it! I would suggest you build a website for your business and post items that you can ship to customers. This is a new day and time, and people would prefer to online shop now instead of get in a car, drive to an actual store, get out, and shop for what they need. They even have services like DoorDash and Postmates where you can have your lunch or dinner delivered right to your door now. Convenience is what consumers want more than anything.

Ok. You have your business name, business license, business checking account, business location, and website. That is great! Now the BIG question is... How are you going to tell the WORLD that you are open for business? Please do not tell me that you are NAÏVE like I was when I opened my very first bakery. I thought because I had exhausted all my savings and paychecks to open Tippy Cakes Bakery that people from all over the city and surrounding cities would come running in flocks to visit my bakery. That is a dream we get from television shows like *DC Cupcakes* and *Cake Boss*. Do not believe the hype, that is for television purposes only.

I was so devastated when I had my very first grand opening and only a handful of people came to visit my bakery. *"How could this be?"* I thought. After all, Harlem, Georgia needed a bakery other than the local IGA grocery store. Let's just say it took some time and money to build my audience and my clientele. The good news is, once you build your clientele and your customer service is as good as your product, you're in the game.

I pride myself on customer service. I would like to place myself on the same level as Chick-fil-A's customer service, and I train and teach my workers the same. You must always greet your customers with a smile. My customers are what keep me in business. I don't care if God blesses me to have 5 Tippy Cakes Bakeries; I will always treat each customer as if they are the most important customer in the world because, to me, they are! They are my bread and butter. They are what keeps my doors open and my lights on. They are my drive to want to do better and keep my bakery open. They were my drive for writing this book! You must take into consideration that without your clients, customers, and consumers, you will not have a business. Pride yourself on giving the best customer service with each transaction, and it will become second nature to you. When your customers are satisfied with your product and customer service, they will want to tell all their family and friends about your business. As a matter of fact, they will make your work easier because they will bring their family and friends right to your door. I love when my customers come to my bakery with someone new and they tell me, "I told them they have to try your desserts; they are so good." That really makes my day!

Let me give you my bluebook on how I built my audience and clientele. It is quite simple, but you must be willing to put in the work! (Grab your highlighter)

Tippy's Clientele Building Checklist

1. Order business cards. I prefer Vistaprint.com or Uprint.com. Both are affordable and the turnaround rate is pretty quick.

2. Purchase a t-shirt with your business name, logo, and contact information (This, my friends, is FREE advertising wherever you go!). You can even sell t-shirts to your customers or do give-a-ways so that they can advertise for you also!

3. Give customers postcards or business cards with a discount or giveaway printed on them. For example: Buy one cake pop, receive one free. Buy one cupcake, receive one half off.

4. Choose a Networking Day (This should always be one of your off days or your slowest working day.) I will go into detail about what you should be doing on your Networking Day later.

5. Post something about your business EVERY DAY on social media. I do not care if your friends and family are tired of seeing or hearing about your business. We are on social media to do one thing: MAKE MONEY!

6. Ask your family and friends to share your business on their social media pages and give some type of incentive to the ones who do share your page. It can be a discount or a buy-one-get-one-free product. You can also do a free raffle to the person who shares your page the most! (This works really well!)

7. If you have a website, sign up for Google Ads and Yelp to add a free listing for your business.

8. Purchase a decal for your vehicle. It can be a small one on your side window, or a medium to large sized one on your back window. You should advertise your business wherever you go.

9. Get an account on Canva.com so that you can create professional templates to post on social media. It makes a world of difference!

10. Post a business ad in your local newspaper.

11. Contact your local radio station and ask about after-hours ad spots (they are normally cheaper, meaning you can get more ad time for your money).

12. Post a Facebook Live or video on your social media page. Customers like to interact and see what you are doing in your business. It could be you describing a product or service that your business offers or a video of you making something. Post videos, ask questions, and keep your customers engaged.

13. Ask for referrals. Do not be afraid to ask your friends or customers on your social media page to share or refer their friends to your business page. Once again, you can offer an incentive.

Let us chat a little about "Networking Day." I try to set out a day at least once a week to network. What I normally do on my Networking Day is: grab lots of business cards, postcards, and samples, and I visit local businesses in my area that I would like as future customers. For example: I will bake up mini cupcakes, sugar cookies, or cake pops and take them to the local schools with a handful of business cards and postcards. I also visit the local hospitals, banks, police departments, courthouses, apartment complexes etc. You are building a relationship with local businesses, and almost nine times out of ten, they will order from you in the future and stop by to visit your business. You do not have to visit all these places at once, but make sure to make a note in your business notebook or journal to visit these places ASAP.

Another thing I do on my Networking Day is visit a big retailer (Walmart, Target, and local grocery stores are always great places to go). I put on my Tippy Cakes t-shirt, I grab a handful of business cards, and I hand out a business card to everyone I come in contact with. I know, I too used to hate walking up to random people, but remember you are a business owner now, so you must get over your fear and become a people person. This is my short script I use when passing out my business cards: "Hello, I am the owner of Tippy Cakes Bakery and I was hoping I could give you a business card, thank you!" One little sentence. You do not have to go into detail because all your information will be on your business card, and if they need your services, they will give you a call. You can also ask your family and friends to pass out your business cards as well. My husband is great at passing out my business cards at work. You will be surprised how many people have been like, "Yes, I was meaning to come visit your bakery," or "I have been looking for someone to make my kid's birthday cake." Now it is a win-win situation for everyone. You have saved someone's day because you have a service or product that they were looking for!

Networking Day will be a game changer for your business. If you do this right, you will notice your customer base growing in no time. You can also join different business owners/entrepreneur groups on Facebook. You also have the local online yard sales on Facebook. I post on those at least once a day to let the locals in my city know the cupcake flavors I am selling for the day. This is FREE advertising. It has brought me so many new customers!

Now that you have my Clientele Building Cheat Sheet, you should be ready to go out and network in your community or with the world and start building your clientele. To get started, we are going to need some yummy sugar cookies to pass out to your new potential customers!

Tippy's Sugar Cookie

2 sticks butter softened

2 cups granulated sugar

2 eggs

1 tsp almond vanilla flavoring

1 ½ tsp baking powder

4 cups all-purpose flour

1 tsp creamer / sprinkles (optional)

Preheat oven to 325 degrees Fahrenheit, prepare baking sheets with parchment paper. Mix butter and sugar, then add eggs one at a time, add almond vanilla flavoring. Whisk baking powder and all-purpose flour together, add to the mixture. You can add sprinkles to the batter if you would like sprinkled sugar cookies. Bake until golden brown, 10 minutes or so. Let cool before taking off baking sheet. You can put cookies in a cellophane bag and tie with a ribbon to make it look decorative and pretty. You can also use a hole puncher to punch a hole in your business card and add it to the string you tie the bag with.

Chapter 3: Strawberry Delight (Building Your Faith)

We have covered a lot of information in these short three chapters, and I hope you are just as excited as I am about you starting, or wanting to start, your business. I can hear some of you in the background saying, "Honey, how do we go about getting money to fund this dream?" Good question, there are multiple ways you can go about funding your dreams. You can use your money from your nine-to-five job, use your savings account, apply and almost max out your credit cards, ask your spouse, boyfriend, girlfriend, or friends and family for money, create a fundraiser, apply for a loan from your bank or credit union, start a Go Fund Me account, find an investor. and so on and so on. I am not here to shoot your dreams out of the sky with negativity because I know how it feels to be so excited about your dreams until someone comes along with the words, "I don't know… are you sure that's going to work?" It makes you second-guess everything you have worked hard for.

I will be realistic with you, when going to a bank to receive funding for a business, they are going to want to see 1-2, or even 3, years of bank statements, tax returns and proof of income. If you are like me, my dream of opening a bakery was just that--a dream. I did not have proof that I was selling a thousand dollars' worth of cupcakes (at least not then) to show to a bank. As a matter of fact, I didn't even have much income from baking because it was a dream of mine, and probably just like you, in the beginning, I was not charging my worth. I was basically giving away my products.

Looking back on it now, because my bakery was a dream--a vision I had had for so long-- and because I wanted everyone to like my product and what I had to offer, when people would order from me, I was selling my products as cheap as possible because I was worried about those customers going to someone else, and guess what... I got BURNT OUT really quick. You must learn in the early stages of planning your business what kind of clients you want and what kind of income you would like to make. Would you rather have one hundred customers ordering your $4-$10 cupcakes or 35 people ordering your $30 a dozen cupcakes? I choose to make high-quality products so that I can cater to customers who do not mind paying what I request versus people trying to nickel and dime me who want something on a discount or for free. That is what Walmart, Food Lion, BI-LO, Ingles, and some other bakeries are for. You must take pride in your craft. Once you start taking pride in your craft and knowing your worth, your whole mindset will change.

This is the chapter where we will talk about FAITH. I'm not talking about my favorite R&B singer Faith Evans, I'm talking about FAITH, when you want something so bad, but you have no idea how you are going to make it happen type of Faith. Honey, I have enough faith built up inside of me to lend everyone who reads this book some. I have enough Faith in me to trust and believe everything I set my heart's desires and mind to will come to fruition because I have a FAITH PLAN. Faith is what got me my first and second bakery. Faith is how I opened a bakery with less than a thousand dollars to my name, Faith is what allowed me to write this book even when I had no clue as to how to write a book.

Do you want to know about my FAITH PLAN? Normally, I write my Faith Plans down in my journal and keep them to myself, but you're in super luck today because I feel super generous. I truly want you to succeed so that one day, I can read your book or see the Grand Opening of your business on Facebook and I can say, "SEE WHAT FAITH CAN DO?!" So, unless you just have money in the bank waiting for you to go to the ATM and withdraw it as a lump sum and start this bakery, I suggest you grab your highlighter or pen.

Whatever higher power you believe in, whether it is God, Jehovah, Allah, Messiah, your Ancestors, or even yourself, this is the time to start showing gratitude. This part is simple. When you wake up in the morning, thank your higher power for your bakery. No, I am not crazy, I know you do not have the physical business yet but start thanking your higher power daily.

The next thing you want to do is close your eyes and envision yourself inside your new bakery/business. Envision every detail of your business starting from the color on the walls. Does the floor have carpet, hard wood floors, concrete, tile, etc.? What does your air freshener smell like? What kind of portraits will be on the walls? How big is your display case? Do you have a counter with a cash register? You get the picture, right? Envision this whenever you are meditating and grab your business journal and write down your visions, your thoughts. How does your vision make you feel? Write all of this down and remember to THANK YOUR HIGHER POWER DAILY.

I am a big advocate of vision boards. I cannot STRESS this enough to my family and friends. Every time I come up with an idea to open a business, I always add it to my vision board. I recently looked at my vision board that is on my side of the bed on my wall so that I could be reminded daily of my dreams and goals, and I was amazed that I had completed a lot of my dreams. I know you have probably heard the saying a thousand times: write the vision, make it plain. You have heard this saying a thousand times because it truly works! Once you write your visions down, it is like a magical signal goes up to the heavens and lets your guardian angel know that you are praying for a miracle of starting and opening your very first business.

I truly believe you cannot expect to start a business or venture if you do not have a plan, a vision. Write it down, make it plain. I once read or was told that when you have a vision or plan, and you pray about it; it is not up to YOU to make that vision or plan come into fruition. Yes, you read that right. It is not up to YOU to make it happen. Let me break this down for you. This is where your FAITH kicks in. Let me go a little more into detail.

Before I opened my second bakery. I had gone through a HORRIFIC divorce, I'm talking about the type of divorce where I really prayed to God that my ex-spouse would run off the road and his truck would catch on fire and get burned up or he would choke on a sip of water and magically die, but with prayer, therapy and more prayer, and lots of repentance, I no longer want my ex dead. I have actually forgiven him and myself (that's another book in itself). I was somewhat broke, and I ended up moving back home from Savannah, Georgia. I had to move back in with my parents at 37 after I had initially moved out on my own when I was 18—talk about depressed and humiliated! This is where my FAITH stepped in: as I was going through all of this, and I was sure my life was going to come to an end. I had to pay over $4,000 for a nasty divorce settlement and pay my ex-husband child support because my son did not want to move to Savannah, Georgia with me. Although it was difficult, I never gave up on my dreams and my visions. As a matter of fact, it brought me closer to God. Those nights that I was all alone and crying myself to sleep in my one-bedroom apartment--in a city where I did not know anyone but one other person--were when I started writing letters to God asking him to deliver me and to help me regain everything that I had lost. When I did that, I stopped crying as much and started feeling less alone.

Although I was grateful for being able to move back in with my parents for four months, it was my mission every day to save up enough money from my part-time job to be able to get my own place. Although my son lived with his father full-time and my daughter was in college, I was still a mother of two. I had to have my own place so that I could provide for my children.

I was so thankful when I received a phone call for a part-time job teaching cosmetology in the afternoons at the same cosmetology school I attended twenty years ago (Look at the Power of God!!), and I started working in a hair salon during the daytime. It wasn't long before I was able to get my own apartment, and although it was nothing major, that two-bedroom townhouse felt like a mansion to me because I had accomplished a goal on my vison board: getting my own place.

After being back in my hometown for a little over a year, I was introduced to my now husband Kevin through a neighborhood friend who I called my big brother, Cordell. Kevin and Cordell had been friends for *way* over ten years. As a matter of fact, I had seen Kevin a few years back when I was married to my ex, and with a quick glance I thought he was cute but didn't give it a second thought. So, when I was living in Savannah, after moving and while waiting for my divorce to be final, I had a conversation with my big brother Cordell, and Kevin's name came up. I asked how Kevin had been and if he was married yet; Cordell replied, "NO. He is not married." So, jokingly, I told Cordell to tell Kevin to call me.

Never in a million years did I think I would now be married to such a sweet soul. Kevin is the answer to all my prayers. Seriously. If you look at my list and description of the man I was praying for, Kevin fits it perfectly, except for one thing… I did not write, "Caucasian male," on that list. I guess God has a sense of humor, but I am so glad that we took a chance on each other, and the rest is history. We are the Holleys, happily married and each other's best friends.

When we decided to get married, we discussed whether we would have a big wedding for family and friends or choose to take the thousands we would spend on a wedding and buy our forever home and help me start a business. Of course, I jumped on the idea of me starting a business!! It was like my prayers had been answered and we did just that!

Remember earlier in this chapter when I said, "It is not up to YOU once you pray for what you're praying for"? Before I even moved back home from Savannah two years later, God, my Guardian Angels and my Ancestors had already aligned mine and Kevin's paths to run across each other. We just had to be at the right place, at the right time, and boom, the magic began! You ever heard the saying, "when our stars align"? That is exactly what happened. Our stars aligned, and baby, we made fireworks! Have you ever had something happen in your life, and you just looked up at the skies and smiled because you knew if it wasn't for a higher power there was no way you could have achieved what you did? It is all about that powerful word FAITH. I am not going to say that everything was super easy for opening my bakery, but it was doable with FAITH, HOPE, and a VISION.

I can tell you that I got frustrated when we had to pay over five hundred dollars just for plumbing for a three-compartment sink, or how I had to have three different inspections, and every time I got excited that I would receive my business license that day, there were one or two more things that needed to be done in order to pass inspection. But when the day came that the inspector finally signed off on my inspection, I shouted, *"Hallelujah, Praise the Lord!"* So, my word of advice to you is if you do not have a lot of patience, get you some and quick! But that is one of the reasons for me writing this book; so that I can save you some headache and help you be better prepared for opening your bakery.

Like I stated earlier, I am not sure for other states, but I am pretty sure they are similar if not the same. The first thing you will want to do once you have found your perfect location is visit your local city hall and request a business license. They will most likely give you a checklist of the things you will have to open. For a bakery in the state of Georgia, you will need an inspection from Georgia Agriculture and your local Health Department. Visit agr.georgia.gov and click on the forms link, under the forms link, click on "Food Sales Establishment License Application." You can print the application out, complete it, and mail it in. Once, they have received your application, they will contact you for an inspection date, so make sure you have the lease and keys to the location you will be operating your business at ready.

Some of the main things you will need for your business are: a three-compartment sink (I purchased mine from Amazon, but also check Facebook market place or other yard sale platforms), a powered exit sign for both doors of your business (also ordered from Amazon), a convection oven (purchased from Facebook Market place) a refrigerator to keep your eggs and milk cold, and a freezer to store your frozen goods. You may also want to purchase a display case to hold your baked goods or a commercial refrigerator/freezer for your retail products.

You will save a ton of money--I am talking about thousands of dollars--if you buy your commercial equipment preowned. Once again, check Facebook marketplace, eBay, online yard sales etc. People are posting and selling things all the time. Even if you can afford to purchase brand new equipment, save that money for a rainy day in your checking account. Trust me. There will be other things to spend money on like: 2 business licenses, fire inspections, plumbing, advertising & etc.

Those are just a few things to get started, but even more importantly, you'll need to stock your inventory. You will have cake boxes, sugar, flour, butter, eggs, milk, buckets of icing, and so much more. I suggest that you join a membership at Sam's Club or Costco, you can even set up a business account with US Foods or Sysco. They are wholesale companies for commercial businesses that will deliver products to you. Once you have your EIN number and business license, you can visit their websites and fill out an application. I frequent Aldi grocery store and Walmart as well when I do not have time to wait for a delivery. I also purchase most of my cake boxes and boards from www.webstuarantstore.com and my bags and cupcake liners from www.papermart.com. You can also google other places that offer the products that you need. There are hundreds of cake supplier companies on the website, and sometimes I shop from them as well. You may even be lucky enough to have a local cake supply shop in your neighborhood and that is perfect! Trust me, there is not just one store we bakery owners purchase from. Just try to buy in bulk so that it will save you money in the long run.

Whew, that was a lot of information to obtain, but the good news is you purchased this book so that you can go back to this chapter whenever you need to! Now that you have all this information to process, are you ready to bake this Strawberry Delight Cake? You can turn it into cupcakes too if you want! I tend to retain information better when I have a sweet dessert on my plate!

Tippy's Strawberry Delight

2 ½ cups self-rising flour

1 tsp baking soda

3 eggs

1 cup of oil

1 ½ cups of sugar

1 cup fresh chopped strawberries

1 tsp strawberry extract or flavoring

1 cup buttermilk

Tippy's Strawberry Cream Cheese Icing

1 8oz package of cream cheese

1 stick of butter

1 ½ bags of confectioners' sugar

1 ½ tsps. strawberry extract or flavoring

¼ cup of heavy whipping cream (may need more if mixture is too thick)

Cream butter and package of cream cheese together. Next, add confectioners' sugar a little at a time until all is added, add 1 ½ tsps. of strawberry extract or flavoring, add heavy whipping cream to your liking. If you are using a standing mixer, mix for at least 5 to 6 minutes until the icing is light and fluffy. Set aside or refrigerate until ready to ice cake or cupcakes.

Preheat oven to 340 degrees Fahrenheit. You will need two separate bowls. In one bowl, place your 2 ½ cups of self-rising flour & 1 tsp baking soda, whisk together and set to the side. In the second bowl, cream 1 ½ cups of sugar and 3 eggs together, add cup of chopped strawberries and tsp of strawberry flavoring, then add 1 cup of oil & buttermilk. Lastly, add your flour mixture to the bowl, mix thoroughly and place in 2 greased 9' cake pans or fill cupcake liners and bake for 20-25 minutes.

Chapter 4: Georgia Peach (Boosting Your Positivity)

I would like to recommend that you read *You Are a Badass At Making Money: Master the Mindset of Wealth* by author Jen Sincero. This book helped me change my mindset about money and made me more appreciative of the money I do have as well as the money that is going to come to me. I do not look at money as the root of all evil, I never have. One thing's for sure, money is what makes the world go around, and to whoever said that money can't buy you happiness, you can happily send it to my bank account, and I will show you what happiness is. Having money to pay my bills on time or before the due date is what makes me happy! Having money to buy the products I need for my bakery is what makes me happy! Having enough money to open a bakery without a bank loan is what makes me happy! Having money to take a vacation with my family makes me happy! You get the picture, right? Do me a favor, jot down 5 things about money that make you happy! And write down this money mantra and say it EVERY SINGLE DAY of your business planning: "I am a Money Magnet; I attract Money and it attracts me!" Say it and believe it! Write this mantra in your business journal, on your vision board, and everywhere else you will see daily.

This chapter will be all about boosting your positivity! I will give you mantras and quotes that helped me along the way. They helped for the days I felt like giving up or got frustrated because I was not generating enough sales. I found these mantras posted by Meteor Baumgart on the internet. I hope they can help you when you need them the most. Write them in your business journal so that you can read them whenever you're having one of those "O' I don't know" moments.

- ❖ *Do not downgrade your dream just to fit your reality, upgrade your conviction to match your destiny.*
- ❖ *Failure is the opportunity to begin again more intelligently.* I really like this saying. When I opened my bakery for the second time, I had so much more knowledge than I had before. I knew what did not work for me the first time, so I did things differently, and, so far, things are working pretty well for me. Listen, just because you may have tried a business before and it wasn't as successful as you had hoped to be or you had to close it before you even got the chance to know if it would be successful, that is ok. You cannot treat a failed business as defeat, it is just merely a small bump in the road. You have to pick yourself up and start again. You will never know your potential if you never try again.

❖ *Sometimes you just have to look back at your past and smile about how far you've come.* Now this is one I do on a regular basis. I like to reflect, not on my past failures but just on how far God has brought me. You can even think back on what you were doing last year around this time. I am sure you are further along today, than you were last year. If you feel you are at a standstill, it is time for you to try something different.

Writing in my personal and business journal helps me on so many levels. It helps me write out my road map of where I would like to see myself in the next week, month, year, five years and so on. I would love to own a boat and a lake house one day, so I write in my visions in my journal and I also reflect on my business and what I would need to do to make this an accomplishment. You can start off small. Say you want to make an extra $200 or $500 for the upcoming week. What I would do is calculate and divide how many of each product I would need to sell in my bakery to make this goal a reality. For example: If I would like to make an additional $200 for the week, I could break it down with a few products. Brownies $2.50 ea. X 80 = $200; 6" Mini Cakes $20ea. X 10 = $200. So, I know I need to cell at least 80 Brownies or 10 Mini Cakes. I could even go a little further and divide my 80 Brownies and sell 40 Cupcakes and 40 Brownies to make my extra $200 dollars.

The next thing I would do is come up with a game plan on how I am going to sell these brownies, cupcakes, or mini cakes without lowering my prices. I would go to www.canva.com and create a pretty template with a picture of the product I would like to sell, then I would post it on my all of my social media outlets that I am having a sale on these items. When people hear or see the word SALE they come running! You can post the sale for a few days or have one set day to host your sale. You can even set up an event on your Facebook page hosting your sale. This normally works for me, but if for some reason you're not selling your products as fast as you'd like, you can always do the "Girl Scouts" approach and go to different local businesses and ask if it is ok to sell your products to the customers that are visiting there. Beauty salons, barbershops, nail salons, car dealerships, hospitals etc. Make sure to have your business cards on hand so that they can contact you for future desserts.

Positive Affirmations

- ❖ Decide what you want.
- ❖ Believe that you can have it!
- ❖ Believe you deserve it and believe it is possible for you!
- ❖ Visualize having what you want, embrace the feeling of already having it!
- ❖ Release to the Universe your gratitude.
- ❖ Treasure your time.
- ❖ Do not fall in love with potential.
- ❖ Be patient.
- ❖ Do not procrastinate.
- ❖ Be hopeful.
- ❖ I am excited about my new beginning.
- ❖ I am enough!
- ❖ I have a lot to offer!
- ❖ Everything is unfolding as it is supposed to.
- ❖ I can find happiness in any situation.
- ❖ I am grateful for the lessons.
- ❖ I choose happiness, health, wealth, and harmony.
- ❖ I am free to be the best version of me!
- ❖ I am allowing myself to feel joy!

Chapter 5: Choc Me Baby (How Bad Do You Want Your Business to Succeed?)

The question I am about to ask you may sound silly or far-fetched but here it goes… How BAD do you want your business to succeed? I have another question. How BAD do you want this business? The reason that I ask this question is because unless you just have a boatload of money stashed in the bank, it's going to take some real dedication to bring your dream of owning a business into fruition. I mean A LOT of dedication, sacrifice, determination, and self-discipline. That new Coach bag that just went on sale? DON'T EVEN THINK ABOUT IT/ Those new Nike AirMax or VaporMax… Yep you get the picture NOPE, NADA, NOT RIGHT NOW. You will need to learn how to SAVE, SAVE, SAVE. I can help you with this.

The first thing I started to do was save all my loose change in my wallet. Whenever, I would make a purchase in a store or anywhere, the change I received, I would put into my change jar. You will be surprised how fast change adds up. The second thing I did was open a Stash account and signed up for the "Round Up" option they offered. This came in handy because every time I made a purchase with my debit card, they would stash my change into an account to round my purchase up to the nearest dollar. For example: If my purchase total were $5.40, they would put .60 cents into my savings account to make the purchase an even $6.00 pretty cool right? I thought so too!

Another tactic you can try is the "Envelope Savings Challenge." You will choose a set amount and put this amount into your envelope every week until you have achieved the maximum amount you want to save. For example: I would put $5 in my envelope per week until I had saved up $100, and once I completed that goal, I would boost it up to a higher amount and before long I had a nice nest egg. But you must be disciplined and not reach into your envelope when you are having a rough week. I like the Stash savings a whole lot better because I can't just reach into my change jar or my envelope savings.

You can even get your spouse or partner to participate and help you save money towards your business goal. I also stopped eating out as much, and trust me, that was a really hard task for me to do because I LOVE eating out. I love my Olive Garden, Chipotle, Applebee's, Chop House, Chick-fil-A, Bojangles (I love the kids chicken supreme meal with fries and a sweet tea; I would eat that at least once a week). So, you get the picture, I LOVE to eat out. Don't get me wrong, I can cook a mean herb baked chicken dish and my son LOVES my pot roast, but when I'm out and about or busy working, sometimes it's easier for me to run to a restaurant drive thru and grab some take out. But when it was time to make this bakery a REALITY I had to start cooking more and fill my little Tupperware dishes with my herb baked chicken, yellow rice, & green beans. Once I started making that a habit, not only was I losing a little weight, but my pockets were getting a lot bigger.

From time to time, I would treat myself and my family to a nice sit-down dinner at one of my favorite restaurants, but the best investment me and Kevin could have ever made was our little black deep freezer. I took pride in going to the grocery stores or Sam's club and stack up on meats and veggies to cook. My mother-in law gifted us an InstaPot, and that thing is AMAZING. I can slow cook soo many things in our InstaPot, it really makes cooking soo much easier. My mother gifted us an air fryer, and, Honey, you cannot tell me I do not make the best thing next to Chinese chicken wings. I have a special recipe I used to soak my chicken wings for a few hours or overnight in that includes ginger, soy sauce, and brown sugar. They are amazing, full of flavor and sticky the way Chinese chicken wings used to be in the little red bag. Yes, I miss those wings, but my recipe is as close to it as it can be!! So, once again, if you don't know how to cook, this would be the perfect opportunity to try some of those yummy recipes you have been browsing on Pinterest, or you need to learn how eat out on a budget, and I can help you with that as well!

When I first moved to Savannah, Georgia and was on a limited budget, until I started receiving my paychecks from teaching, I was a fan of the 4 for 4 at Wendy's. Or I would get a small garden salad, six piece nuggets and an ice water for a little over $3.00. I would also get a kids meal from McDonald's, a one entree bowl from Panda Express with the Orange Chicken and rice with some broccoli for a little over $6, two beef Chalupa Supremes for five dollars and some change at Taco Bell, and let's not forget about the famous 1 breast meal at KFC with a side and sweet tea for $5. You can send me a restaurant and I bet I can give you a cheap meal plan! Even if I broke down and brought an $8.31 Cobb salad from Chick-fil-A or an $8.00 one from Zaxby's, I knew how to split my salad in half so I could eat half during my meal and half later. So, you get the picture I used to eat out quite a bit.

I am thankful for my chapters of struggling because it taught me how to appreciate the little things I had. So, when God blessed me with bigger things (and He did bless me), I would appreciate them more. I know what it feels like to sleep on an air mattress in a one-bedroom apartment, or better yet, what it feels like to sleep in different hotels for about a month straight until I was able to afford my deposit and first month's rent on my one-bedroom apartment. I look back now and say, *"Thank You God,"* because even though I was going through a rough patch, a divorce, and living in a city where I didn't know but one other person, God and the Universe were preparing me for my road to success, and that is enough news to make me want to jump up shout and do the shoulder lean! LOL yes, I am Old School! I still play Young Dro

"Shoulder Lean" til this day, it is on my bakery playlist whenever I need some hype music to get me in the zone to be super productive.

So, I told you all about me sleeping on an air mattress in my one-bedroom apartment to let you know that "tough times don't last forever." You must learn how to pray and praise your way out of any situation you are faced with. Honey, when I was in my little one-bedroom apartment, I would get on my knees, and I would pray and thank God for what he was bringing me through. I would write letters to God and tape them in my closet like the movie *War Room*. I would write my dreams and aspirations in my Prayer Journal and tape some of those papers in my closet as well. I did not know how I was going to be successful, but Honey, I had FAITH, a VISION, a GAME PLAN, and a PRAYER LIFE.

I cried and prayed, prayed and cried, and my God came through for me time and time again. It wasn't long before I went from having only the little money I had left from selling all of my stuff when I closed my bakery back in Harlem, Georgia to receiving not one paycheck, but two paychecks from both of the jobs I was blessed with while living in Savannah, Georgia. I taught at Virginia College in the daytime and at Empire Beauty at nighttime. I was exhausted working two jobs, Monday through Thursday (I would have Fridays off at Empire Beauty unless they needed me to sub for another instructor), but it was totally worth it. It gave me the chance to get on my feet, pay off my old bills and credit card debt, and even afford a $4,000 divorce, so, before you come at me with, "Tiff, you just don't understand what I've been through," actually, I do. There is so much more I could put into this book about hard times, heartache, and pain, but hey, who is reminiscing on the past? Not me! I can only look back on some of the things I have been through--and put myself through--and just say, *"Thank God the light bulb finally clicked and I finally learned the lesson that God, the Universe and Mother Earth were trying to teach me."* When you learn to get to a happy place on your own, that is a wonderful thing. So, my words to you are: *You are Amazing, you have more power than you think you have, and it is time to let your bright light shine for others to see.* I pass the torch to you! It is time for you to tell your amazing story and motivate others. By the end of this book, I hope that I have been a motivation to you, and I hope that you will be excited to jumpstart your business, even write a book, start a motivating Facebook group, and so much more!!

Writing this book was therapy for me. It is currently 12:19 AM, and I'm up writing this chapter because I feel that someone out there may need a little encouraging, a little push. They may need to hear from someone who did not come from a rich background or from someone who didn't have their shit together. But guess what, ANYTHING is possible, if you just BELIEVE. If you do not BELIEVE in yourself, why should someone else believe in your dreams? When you write your vision for your business, I should be able to envision your eyes bright and wide open with the biggest grin on your face because you should be so excited and bursting open with sprinkles when you are discussing your business, and if you are not bursting with sprinkles, maybe that is not your dream business. Revamp and think about what really make you happy and excited, and picture yourself running that business. Remember the famous saying "write it down, make it plain." You must envision your success and you have to truly believe it will come to pass.

True story: Anyone who TRULY knows me, knows that a Black Mercedes Benz GLK 350 was/is my dream vehicle. Ever since I was in my early twenties, maybe even before then, I always dreamed or pictured myself driving down the highway in my GLK 350. I put this vehicle on my vision boards along with my pictures of my house, my rental property, my boat, business ventures, marriage goals, and weight loss goals. These things on my vision board were what success meant to me. I felt if I finally had my GLK 350 I had reached a level of success. Well... Guys... I have finally hit that level of success! Now I have to complete another vision board or add onto the one I have. I have currently accomplished almost everything on my vision board (except my boat and my rental property), so guess what? I will go super hard to make sure those things will come to pass, Lord willing. And I have to question my boat on my vision board because I have been on several cruises, so maybe that is what it meant on my vision board because I didn't write "own a boat." Remember, write the vision, make it plain. I did not write that part, so if that's the case I have brought that vision into fruition several times by going on cruises and dinner boats. Now I have to work on this rental property dream of mine. Who is with me?

Chapter 6: Tippy's Red Velvet

Baking with Tippy Cakes!

Tippy's Red Velvet Recipe

2 1/2 cups all purpose flour
1/4 cup cocoa powder
1 teaspoon salt
1 1/2 cup oil
1 1/2 cups granulated sugar
2 eggs
1 bottle (1 oz) red food coloring
1 1/2 teaspoons vanilla
1 Cup buttermilk
1 teaspoon baking soda

Cream Cheese Icing

1 pkg Cream Cheese
2 1lb bags powdered sugar
stick butter
small package Crisco shortening
Heavy Whipping Cream

This is one of the templates that I used for free on canva.com since they have hundreds of templates that you can use and all you have to do is insert your pictures and your text, they even have pictures you can use as well. Red Velvet is a southern classic and one of my top sellers at my bakery. Very simple to make but very sweet, moist, and tasty!

My Special Recipe _____

- ❖ _____ Eggs
- ❖ _____ Cup/Cups Sugar
- ❖ _____ Cups of Flour
- ❖ _____ Cups of Butter/Oil
- ❖ _____ Teaspoons of Baking Soda
- ❖ _____ Cups of Milk/Water
- ❖ _____ Teaspoons of Flavoring
- ❖ _____ Teaspoons of Baking Powder
- ❖ _____ Salt
- ❖ _____
- ❖ _____
- ❖ _____
- ❖ _____

Now describe how we will make this special recipe:

Chapter 7: Granny's Apple Pie (The Reason Why You Love to Bake)

I can close my eyes and remember when my Grandmother Amy was alive. My Grandmother was one of the best cooks I have ever known, and I am so blessed and fortunate that she passed down her great genes of cooking to my mother, my Aunt Marie, and Aunt Sherry. I can remember on Sundays after church service my grandmother's house was the place to be. The house would be filled with my mother, aunts, uncles, my siblings, all my cousins, and other family members from church. Everyone loved my grandmother's cooking; she could make the best fried chicken. The crust on her fried chicken would always be golden brown every time. She was famous for her spicy dressing, fried corn, collard greens, and macaroni and cheese. Just thinking about my grandmothers cooking is making me hungry. What I loved most from my grandmother were her desserts. Her yellow cake with homemade chocolate icing was my favorite. Her peach cobbler had the perfect golden crust and the warm peaches with a dash of cinnamon would just melt on your tongue and fall in your stomach like a dessert made from heaven. I even loved her cinnamon apples and apple pie. My Aunt Marie was able to master my grandmother's homemade caramel cake where you actually cook the caramel on the stove and her fried corn and fat back. I have tried my hand at it, but it is nowhere near as delicious as my Grandma Amy. She was also famous for her sweet potato pie, coconut pie, and pecan pie in which my mother can make just like my grandmother. I can remember staying at my grandmother's house during the daytime in the summer and I could smell her cooking when me and my cousins were outside playing, those were the good ole days and I'd do anything to go back to those days where I could taste my grandmother's cooking. I even loved my grandmother's lima beans, field peas, and black-eyed peas. I could eat just the vegetables with cornbread by itself. And how could I forget about her pound cakes, Lord have mercy on my soul, if you were ever lucky to eat a piece of her pound cake hot out the oven, then you have already tasted a piece of heaven. It was a miracle how she could cook these big elaborate meals on Sunday and feed so many people.

If you mention Amy Williams around my family, they will start reminiscing on how good my grandmother could cook. She did not just pass her cooking skills down to her daughters; my mother and my two aunts, she also passed it down to my three uncles as well. It seemed like my grandmother could make a meal out of anything.

My mother has taken on the role of my grandmother and she now hosts family dinners. I hope to one day keep the tradition going once my mother is no longer living. I pray that will be a hundred years from now. My mother is famous for her red velvet cakes and 7UP pound cakes. She can bake these cakes with her eyes closed and they will come out moist and perfect every time. I have to perfect these two cakes from her soon, I have tried and tried and don't get me wrong, they are pretty good and I sell a great deal of them, but they are nowhere near as moist and delicious as my mother's.

We have a funny superstition in our family, if you are a woman and you are baking a cake, you are not supposed to have sex the night before, if you do have sex the night before you bake a cake, you are supposed to cross your legs before you place the cake into the oven or your cake will not rise. This may be funny, but I promise you if I ever have sex the night before or the morning of baking a cake, you better believe my legs will be crossed before placing my cake in the oven!

Baking is like science, and you have to get familiar with your kitchen. Your kitchen is your safe haven. Your kitchen is where the magic happens. Your kitchen is what brings your family together. Your kitchen brings joy and laughter to you and your loved ones. Do not look at cooking as a chore or job. Look at kitchen as your therapy, how you will heal the world from hunger. Think of your cooking as a gift to others and it will be more enjoyable.

Look up different recipes to try that you would not usually cook. Every couple of weeks I like to do tours of the world, for instance; Monday, maybe a tour to Japan and I will cook Hibachi or Japanese food. Tuesday (if there are no leftovers), I will take my family on a tour to Mexico and I will make taco salad, quesadillas, black rice, or a Mexican dish with seasoned cut up chicken breast and steak with Mexican rice. Wednesday or Thursday, maybe a tour to Italy, and I will cook Italian food. I have an amazing herb baked chicken dish I have been cooking for years, or I may cook a lasagna with warm garlic bread and a salad and other sides, although I LOVE Olive Garden's lasagna a little too much. We make it fun, and everyone looks forward to our tours around the world.

Even when we go out to dinner, we sometimes pick a restaurant no one has ever eaten at, and that can be a challenge because I LOVE to eat out. Don't get me wrong, I love to cook also (at times) but I really love the experience of going out to eat and enjoying a nice conversation with my husband and kids about how their day went, or what do they have planned for the weekend or are there any projects coming up at school that I should be aware of. I love family time, and I love to sit down and eat a nice meal with my family. I also love when we go out to dinner with family, it is fun, and it makes my soul happy. Especially when we take my parents out to eat. My father is so picky, he only loves soul food. In addition to his famous BBQ & Hash that draws crowds of people to his house on holidays, this man will cook collard greens, macaroni and cheese, dressing, sweet potatoes, fried ribs, BBQ ribs, fried or baked chicken, pig feet, and so many other things on any given Sunday. I have had BBQ all over the state of

Georgia and I promise you no one compares to his. I am not saying this because he is my father, this man has a gift!

As I stated earlier in the book, I come from a family of cooks; my father, my mother, my late grandmother, my Aunt Rosie… I could go on and on with family members. My cousin Willie Tutt, I really admire Willie, I believe I have some of his entrepreneur blood running in my veins. Willie is an Army Veteran turned Chef. I loved his passion for cooking, catering, and opening different restaurants. He taught me that just because one business idea does not work, it does not mean to give up on your dream! From time to time, he and his wife Christine, come to visit my bakery and have lunch with me. I cherish my family and I love to hear his old war stories when he was in Vietnam. That is a blessing to have a family member still alive who served in Vietnam.

Chapter 8: Lemon Berry (The Beauty of Being an Entrepreneur)

One thing I have noticed in the world today; no one wants to talk about their failures or failed scenarios. I too have run from my failures for years, and it was not until I decided to tackle my failures head on that I was able to move on with my life and HEAL. That is when I met my dear sweet friend Danielle Parks who was a minister at my new church I had recently restarted visiting after moving back home from Savannah. I was such a broken woman looking back over my life. I had recently went through a nasty divorce, I was living at my parents' home, I went from having an extra paycheck every week from teaching at two schools to only having a part-time job, I could go on and on about what wasn't going right in my life until she suggested I started a journal on thanking God for the things that were going right or thanking him for my many blessings. After jotting my blessings down week after week, I started to feel more thankful and appreciative. I started to release my hurt and anger and fuel it into positive energy to help me attain my goals. I started another vision board, and before you know it, I was on my way to a new Tiffany. I would wake up in the mornings with gratitude and thankfulness, I started exercising and eating healthier because I wanted a revenge body (you know the type where you want to look amazingly sexy so whenever your ex saw you, they would regret all the wrong things they have done to you lol). I was able to be there for both my kids, and finally, I was able to start working on my goals and dreams. I could not move forward in my life until I was able to face my demons and tackle on my failures. I truly thank God for my life coach and now dear friend Danielle Parks. She is an angel here on earth!

My first failure was not loving myself enough. I loved my husband and I loved raising my children in a two-parent household. I was raised with both of my parents in the household, and when I got older, I understood the sacrifices my mother made so that this was possible. But I also knew I deserved better. I had to grow up and learn that I was ENOUGH. Have you ever heard the saying, "Hurt people, hurt people"? That was our life, our truth, who we were, and I knew if I wanted a better future, I would have to make a stand for the both of us. Even as painful as I knew it would be, breaking up our home, it had to be done. I started searching on Indeed.com for Cosmetology Educator jobs, and some in Atlanta, Georgia, Savannah, Georgia, and Jacksonville, Florida popped up in my search results. I filled out the job application to the Cosmetology school in Savannah, Georgia not expecting the school to call me, and Lord and behold, they called me two days later asking if I would be interested in coming down for an interview. I secretly drove to Savannah, Georgia for the very first time for the interview and was offered the job on the spot. I asked if I could have two weeks to talk it over with my husband and give her my final answer, she said yes. As I drove back home, I thought of all the reasons that it would be a perfect idea to move to Savannah, Georgia and take the job. It could be a new beginning for my family, new scenery. When I got home, I told him the exciting news and it did not go as planned. He gave me every excuse why he could not go and as I begged and pleaded with him, he said he would think about it. I could hardly sleep that night because I was so excited. I had my mind made up either way. All I could see was a new beginning and new happiness. A week passed by, and he had pretty much made up his mind and stated that he would not be moving to Savannah, so I gave him a better offer. The offer was for me to move to Savannah and teach during the week and come home as often as possible and to work there for a year to save up enough money so that we could buy a home and I could transfer to a cosmetology school closer to our hometown. That was the main reason why I agreed to take the teaching job in Savannah, because no cosmetology schools near me were hiring at the time. I guess everything happens for a reason and I was meant to move to Savannah, Georgia for two and a half years.

This is where my second failure happened; I had previously opened a bakery two years prior to me planning to leave and move to Savannah. Being that it was in a small town, I was barely making ends meet once I paid the rent, utilities, bought product, and so on for the bakery. So, when I got the opportunity to move to Savannah to teach making twenty dollars an hour, I thought why not close the bakery and save up to open another bakery in another city once I move back. That was one of the hardest things I had to do, make an announcement on social media that Tippy Cakes would be closing permanently. The bakery was my baby, I had spent countless nights staying up late baking and decorating cakes, I had met so many new people, did so many wedding and birthday cakes and built quite a clientele, but at the end of the day, it was not enough to take care of my personal expenses, household bills, and the bakery, and let's not forget I had spent most of my savings and income to open this dream bakery of mine. As I began to pack up my belongings in the bakery and sell as much stuff as I possibly could, the tears started to form and roll down my face because I felt like a failure.

I wanted to blame everyone but myself. If only I had enough support from the people in the town, they did not want to support my bakery because I was black. I even blamed my ex-husband for not supporting my bakery financially until I was stable enough to support it on my own. But you know whose fault it was? MINE… I had to swallow that bullet and learn that I was to blame for my bakery not succeeding.

How could I expect to be running over with business in a small town that had a population of less than 3,200 people; sure, all these people were not going to come running to my bakery begging for cakes and cupcakes. I should have saved more money before draining out my savings account to open my bakery. Trust me, I know how hard it is to want to own something so badly that you think you can spend all of your life savings and make it back as soon as you open up the business. Listen to me friend, DO NOT SPEND your life savings only to end up with a closed business and you dead broke. I have seen it time and time again with small businesses. This is not the mistake you want to make. Please save for your business and look at other revenues to fund your business, be it a loan, credit cards, fundraisers etc. This is not an impossible task. I should have waited until my ex-husband and I were financially stable enough to open the bakery instead of me thinking he was hating on my dream and opening it anyway.

There are so many things I can blame myself for. But before I learned all of this in therapy I turned into a bitter person on the inside and all I could see were my failures, not knowing these were just steppingstones to prepare me for another life lesson. Now, looking back on closing my first bakery, I am glad I did. I was working myself raggedy and I was stressed to the max. I could not afford to hire help at the bakery, so I was basically doing everything by myself. Baking, decorating, advertising, networking, doing all the ordering, it is no wonder I did not have a stroke or mini heart attack. And I missed a lot of family moments, my children's softball and baseball games, family cookouts and reunions, my ex-husband's races at the racetrack all because I was struggling to keep the bakery doors open because of my pride. How would I be able to face the people in the city if I had to close my bakery because I could not afford it? Well, the answer is: with my head held high and a damn smile!

What you must learn my friends, is that even if your first business fails, that does not mean you should give up on your dreams. Learn from your past mistakes and try again, but this time, with a blueprint that will help you succeed. There is no need to beat yourself up because your idea or business did not take off like a rocket ship. That is ok, but you know what is even better? Learning how to get up off the ground, dust your shoulders off and get back out there.

I have another friend who had a storefront bakery and had to close her bakery, but instead of giving up on her dreams, she started an online bakery and started baking from home and now her business is doing exceptionally well. It is not all about the brick-and-mortar business, it is just about getting out there and starting from somewhere!

Now, if you plan to open another business and do the same exact thing you did before, you may want to expect another failure, but if you look back over everything that went wrong in your business and critique it, you may be on to bigger and better things. The first city I opened a bakery in had only 3,200 people. My next bakery opened in a city that had over 6,606 people, and that made a whole lot of difference. We must learn from our mistakes and use them as learning lessons, do not cry or pout about it. Look at the NEW Tiffany, I can speak this knowledge because I learned from my mistakes.

At my new bakery, I was able to afford to hire help and it makes a world of difference, I also learned to take days and time off to enjoy my family. If I want to take a mini vacation, I can now because I have reliable help. I also do not work crazy hours or late nights. I do not take on more work than I can handle, and I learned to use the word NO. If I close my bakery at 6pm now, I give myself no longer than 30 minutes to clean and prep for the next day. If it is something that I have not completed, I wrap it up and save it for the next day. I had to learn, it is just cakes, it is not a life-or-death situation, and if someone is not happy about my hours or service, they are more than welcome to visit another bakery.

I look over my past now and I can smile and say, *"Thank you God for delivering me out of my own mess."* I can now look at my ex-husband and laugh and say we were so young and clueless about life. I have a newfound friendship with him. We had to have a heart-to-heart with each other and realize that we still have a young king to raise, and that it is better to work on some things together than against each other. When you learn to grow in life, instead of holding onto the things and people who hurt you; life can be a beautiful thing and although our marriage did not last, at least we have a friendship and a smart, handsome son to share. There was no need for either one of us to hold onto our guilt and anger. You learn these things when you grow as a person. I am thankful that I was able to move to another city and come back home with a new perception on my life. And I am thankful for the people who helped me get to where I am today.

I would like to give a huge thank you to Pastor Andre Osborne at First Tabernacle Baptist Church of Savannah, Georgia. This man welcomed me into his church after visiting a few times and made me feel like I was home. When I was in a city all alone, he and his lovely wife and church members welcomed me and gave me a reason to want to learn more about God and share my time with their church family. To Pastor Andre Osborne, I am very grateful that God put your awesome church in my path, and I will forever be a member even if I live in another city. I loved everything about First Tabernacle, and the church choir is AMAZING. They can heal your soul with their singing and praise. Your prayers are what kept me sane when I thought about taking my own life, and for that, I will forever be grateful to you and your church family.

To my friend Yolanda, I thank you for being my listening ear and my Prayer Warrior when I was going through my chapter of divorce. Just you listening to me vent and cry. or you driving two and a half hours just to come see me and check on me, I am thankful. I love your colorful spirit, you are a joy to be around, never a dull moment with you.

To my beautiful friend Nikki who I met while our sons were playing on the same baseball team, I can't thank God enough for your beautiful spirit, you are a true definition of a sister friend and I hope you think of me as the same. I cannot wait until I make it big so that I can have you travel the world with me. I am still looking forward to our girls' trip to an exotic island just to laugh and toast it up and say that we made it! To my friend Antoinette, aka "Little Firecracker," lol, you are my height (5'2) but you're always ready to pull up, ride up, or snatch somebody up if need be. Thanks for becoming my accidental friend. I love you even though sometimes you dangle on my last good nerve. I would not trade you for the world. You ladies have been there by my side for some dark, difficult days, and I hope to one day repay you for your love and friendship.

I am pretty sure you can think of a few people who you can call and chat with who make you feel better just by a phone call. Learn to call them more or send a quick text message just to tell them you appreciate them, and thank them for being a genuine friend. Friends and family are so needed in our lives. Even when you feel like it is you against the world sometimes, I am pretty sure there is at least one person you can call to talk to and make you feel better. These types of people are precious gems, and I am so thankful to have a few of them in my phone. To this day, I have weekly phone conversations with my father and my mother, I really enjoy our talks, they always make any situation better and I love the fact that I can see and hear their smiles through the telephone. My daughter and I text on a daily basis, even when we are in the same house, she is in her room and I in mine and we text each other silly stuff or she shares one hundred Tik Tok videos every day, but it is my therapy and I really look forward to the text messages and phone calls.

Now, let's make this Lemon Berry Cupcake, one of Tippy Cakes' favorites! Remember you can make this as a cake instead of cupcakes, you will just need to grease and batter two 9" cake pans and bake for at least 25 minutes with the oven set at 340 degrees Fahrenheit. I always wrap my cakes in plastic saran wrap, set in freezer for 30 minutes to an hour before I ice and decorate.

Lemon Berry Cake

1 box of white cake mix

1 cup of sugar

3 eggs

1 cup of all-purpose flour

1 cup of oil

1 ½ cups milk

2 tsp lemon extract

½ cup of blueberries

3-4 drops of yellow food coloring

Tippy's Lemon Buttercream Icing

2 bags of confectioners' sugar

1 stick of butter

1 cup of Crisco shortening

3 teaspoons of lemon extract

¾ cup coffee creamer or heavy whipping cream

Mix shortening, butter together until creamy consistency, slowly add powdered sugar to mixture. Once the mixture is thick and clumpy, slowly add coffee creamer or heavy whipping cream & lemon extract until it is a thick smooth texture. Whip on high for 5 to 10 minutes until light and fluffy.

Chapter 9: Birthday Bash (Getting Excited About Your Business)

So, are you happy yet? Are you Excited about starting or expanding your business? I hope that you are! There is so much information that I want to give you, I keep reading over the past chapters to make sure I have not forgotten anything. Sometimes when I am at work, a thought or idea pops up in my head and I tell myself, *"I have to put this in the book when I get home."* Honestly, a lot of things you will learn by repetition. For example, your favorite recipe. You will learn to add things to it or take things away to make it YOUR favorite recipe. I have seen and tried hundreds of recipes, and the truth of the matter is, a lot of them, if not all of them, have the same basic key ingredients: flour, butter or oil, eggs, baking soda or baking powder, milk, and so on… it's the flavorings and other things you add to the recipe that make it your own. For example: for some of my recipes that require milk, I may use Italian Sweet Crème coffee creamer because, to me, it gives it a richer, sweeter taste. You will learn how to tweak your own recipes. Do not get angry or upset if the recipe does not turn out the way you wanted it to. Just toss the failed product in the trash and start again. I cannot tell you how many dozens of cupcakes I have had to trash because they did not rise, or after halfway baking, I realized I forgot to add the eggs. Yes, this has happened to me more times than I can count, but I do not beat myself up about it.

You must learn to forgive yourself more and not be so hard on yourself. I like to call it my "go passes." I work so hard on not sweating the little things. I try really hard not to get upset about things that I cannot control because at the end of the day, a lot of things we tend to get upset over or about are tedious, and who has time for tedious things? Not I.

My family used to play this silly game where we would designate Wednesday to be our fuss and complain day. Whenever one of the kids would fuss and complain or try to tell on the other one, me and my ex-husband would laugh and say, "Is it Wednesday?" Looking back on it now, I chuckled because although we did it as a funny game, I kind of took on to it and I try to limit my days of fussing and complaining.

Whenever I feel overwhelmed about cake orders, before I complain, I say, *"Thank you God for these customers. Thank you God for Tippy Cakes."* Because if it weren't for the customers ordering cakes, cupcakes, brownies, cake pops, or whatever dessert they need for an event, family function, birthday party, or wedding, I would not have my dream business, working my dream job doing what I love: offering delicious desserts and putting smiles on people's faces. So, do me a favor; go to Walmart, Family Dollar, Dollar General, Hobby Lobby, Michaels, JoAnn's, or any of those cute crafty stores and invest in a nice durable journal, notepad, or notebook. This will be our Thankful & Grateful Journal. I promise this will help you change your outlook on life and the things we so very often take for granted daily. Start off listing ten small things that you are grateful for and why. For example: It could be *"Thank You God or Universe for the toilet tissue in the bathroom so that I do not have to use a washcloth, or worse, my hand to wipe my behind."* Yes, that is a funny one, but you get the picture. Try to make it a habit of writing in your Thankful & Grateful Journal at least once or twice per week, and if you're lucky enough to write in it daily, you are kicking some serious butt! I know it is easier said than done, but honey, DON'T SWEAT THE SMALL STUFF. We are too busy focusing on becoming a successful business owner!! A Boss, A Queen, King, Provider, and all that good stuff!!

That last sentence brings me to a very important question for you. Grab your pen and jot down your answer. What does SUCCESS mean to YOU? Yes, YOU… Remember, I was an Educator for eight years, so I love to ask questions and I do not want you to just jot anything down. I want you to think long and hard about what SUCCESS means to you. The next question I have for you is: Once you have achieved this level of success, will that be enough for you, or will you set a new goal for what success will mean to you?

For starters, ever since I was in my early twenties, I labeled success as: having money in the bank (I never said or wrote down how much, be careful with that one). Remember the saying "write the vison and make it plain?" So, when I only had fifty dollars in the bank, I should have still looked at it as me being successful because all I wrote was "money in the bank" lol. Now you see why it is so important to be very detail oriented when writing your dreams and goals? The next thing is I wanted was a nice house (once again, never stated size, how many bedrooms blah, blah, blah) and a black Mercedes GLK 350. I always had what I would consider a nice house. It was not the mansion I had always dreamed of, but I was blessed to always have a nice house. Let's just say when I got older, like in my mid-thirties, I started being very detailed oriented about what I thought success was to me and the things I wanted to achieve in my successful life.

This is where your vision board will come into play. I live by this, I truly do. I cannot explain it, but you have to manifest your dreams, you have to want it so bad that you cannot sleep at night thinking about it. You have to literally talk it into existence. My husband, parents and kids can vouch for this; I spoke my bakery into existence, but I did not just speak it, I actually put in the hard work to make it a reality, and now I am fortunate enough to tell my story to others who were hopeful like me. I get to show you my blueprint on how I made it possible, and prayerfully, this will give you the motivation you need to jumpstart your plans of starting your own business.

Listen, the saying "Faith without works is dead" is a true statement. Yes, you can have a dream, a vision, and a plan, but you must put in the work. So, you do not have the funds to open a bakery today, ok, that is perfectly fine. Do you have a kitchen? If you do not, I am sure a family member or friend does. You have to start somewhere. I started baking goods in my kitchen and posting pictures on Facebook and passing out business cards to people I knew and also had family members and friends pass out my business cards to their family and friends and that is how I started to build my clientele. There are so many groups and pages on social media that you can showcase your talent and craft to. It is truly amazing, and I really hope you take advantage of social media in a positive way because it can change your life, literally. It changed mine and I will continue using social media to post and advertise about my business for as long as they allow me to.

It is funny, I started writing this book during the COVID-19 pandemic, I was in shelter in place for about two months, and I opened my bakery back up Mother's Day weekend. I grossed over thirteen hundred dollars in two days. I had gone through 120 eggs easily, and literally every month since May, I have been grossing over one thousand a week, or close to it, in my bakery. That was a blessing. It shows that just because there was a pandemic going on, people still wanted what Tippy Cakes had to offer.

I even made it more convenient for them to get their desserts. We delivered and offered to mail and ship certain desserts if they were unable to visit the bakery. The community was amazing at showing love and support to our first responders as well, and I would send donations of cupcakes to the first responders to show my love and appreciation. Remember, customer service and a smile can go a long way.

Also, do not forget about Networking Day, bake up some samples, grab your business card, and go out into the town and introduce yourself and your sweets! You got this and I will be here cheering you on saying, "You can do it!"

And last but not least, recently, I was able to get my Black Mercedes GLK 350, so now I am humbly and gratefully feeling really successful, but you know me, I won't stop there, it is time to start a whole new vision board! I have so many visions and dreams I would like to turn into reality before I pass away on this earth. So many places I want to visit, so many things I want to do and so many blessings I want to bestow upon my parents, husband, kids, family, and friends. I would like to open my second bakery, Lord willing, within the next year or two. So, if you have not already started your vision board, now would be a good time to go purchase some poster board, glue, tape, and magazines.

Vision Board Checklist

- Poster board or Dry Erase Board
- Markers
- Pen
- Colorful Construction Paper or Cardstock
- Hot Glue Gun or Elmer's Glue
- New or Old Magazines (ask friends & family)

Vision Board Ideas

- What does your dream home look like?
- What does your dream car/truck look like?
- What is your dream job?
- How much money would you like to see in your bank account?
- What are your hobbies? What do you like to do for fun?
- Any destinations you would like to visit?
- Anyone you would like to meet?
- If you won the lottery, what would you purchase? Where would you visit?

Those are a few things to get you started on your vision board! Remember, envision yourself doing the things or obtaining the things you have on your board. You are opening a magical airway between your brain and the Universe to manifest all your heart's desires.

My Vision Board Rough draft

Use this page to visualize your vision board. If you would like, you can use this page as your rough draft. Start by writing things you would like to manifest into your life. Write where do you see yourself in the next couple of months, years etc. If you would like to open a business, write down all the things that you would like to have in your business.

Be very specific with your vision board.

Vision Board Rough Draft

What does SUCCESS mean to YOU?

Tippy's Keys to Success!

- Always wake up with a grateful and thankful heart.
- Always start your day with prayer.
- Let the small stuff go.
- React with a smile and love instead of anger.
- Do everything you can to help the next person.
- Be willing to share information--even information that people were not willing to share with you because that is how you get your blessings!
- Give more, smile more!
- Hustle and network everyday
- Most importantly, believe in yourself, believe in your vision, believe in your business!

Now that we are on the right track with manifesting our dreams, it is time to bake up some Birthday Bash Cupcakes, grab a glass of milk, and get to work on those vision boards!

Birthday Bash Cupcakes/Cake

1 ½ cups granulated sugar

1 cup of butter

3 eggs

2 teaspoons vanilla extract

2 ¾ cups all-purpose flour

1 tablespoon baking powder

1 cup buttermilk

2 teaspoons of coffee creamer

Sprinkles (rainbow or bright colored sprinkles) 3 tablespoons

Birthday Bash Buttercream Icing

2 bags of confectioners' sugar

1 stick of butter

1 cup of Crisco shortening

¾ cup coffee creamer or heavy whipping cream

Mix shortening, butter together until creamy consistency, slowly add powdered sugar to mixture once the mixture is thick and clumpy, slowly add coffee creamer or heavy whipping cream until it is a thick smooth texture. Whip on high for 5 to 10 minutes until light and fluffy. Add Sprinkles once texture is light and fluffy.

Chapter 10: Chocolate Espresso (Time to Add Some Heat and Pressure)

Chocolate Espresso is one of my favorite cupcake flavors at Tippy Cakes Bakery, the moisture in the cake is unbelievable and to bite into a super moist chocolate cupcake and taste chocolate chip morsels with a splash of espresso, it's a no brainer why that is one of the most sold cupcake flavors at the bakery, that one and the chocolate espresso. I am a chocolate lover by heart. Something about adding hot water or hot coffee to the cake batter helps set the tone for this chapter.

Let's talk about the word "grit," what it means, and why it is important when trying to open a business. Grit (according to Oxford Languages) means courage and resolve, strength of character. The reason why "grit" will become an important word once you become a business owner is because you will need to have strength of character. You will get tested on all types of levels. Trust me on this one. People will be rude to you, they may be having a bad day already and come to your place of business and take it all out on you, and although in your head you would love to give them a piece of your mind, you will have to bite your tongue, put on a smile and ask how can you fix their situation, even if the problem is not yours to fix.

Prime example: the other day I had a customer who had came into the bakery the previous week and my assistant took her order. The customer wanted a two-tier cake with the top layer lilac and the bottom layer an ombre of purples. I took the order form and proceeded to decorate the top tier a light lilac and the bottom tiers starting off with lilac, a darker lilac, and purple on the bottom. When the customer came to pick up the cake; she was not happy with the colors. She wanted the purples to be a deep dark purple at the bottom. She went on and on about colors and how the other woman should have showed me a picture. I let her get all her frustrations out and asked her how I could rectify the situation. I asked her if she like for me to redo the cake or to refund her. She hesitated for a second and then stated she supposed I could just scrape all the icing off the cake and redo the colors. Well, if you are a professional like I would like to think I am, we know it is not that simple. To make a long story short, I ended up staying at the bakery an additional three hours after closing just to bake another cake to appease the customer. Did I have something planned after work? Sure I did, but those plans had to be postponed because as a business owner, you want to make sure the customer is always satisfied. Believe me, a bad review will go way further than a positive review. I like to pride my bakery on having five-star reviews, and I like to go far and beyond to satisfy my customers. At the end of the day, they are the reason why I am in business.

I'm sure you have had an experience where you spent all night on a cake and it did not turn out the way you intended it to, or you were walking with the cake in your hand and it just magically drops on the floor. Devastating, right? That is part of being a business owner.

Question? You just spent the last six to eight hours baking a cake, decorating the cake to the best of your ability, you truly believe this is one of your master pieces, the customer comes to pick up the cake and tells you that she is not pleased with the cake, it is nothing like what she expected, and she would like to request a refund. Besides crying, what would you do? This could very well happen. Thank God this has never happened to me personally, but things like this happen all the time. This is where grit (remember that definition: your strength of character, courage and resolve) will come in.

Let us talk about resilience for second. What is resilience? Resilience is the capacity to recover quickly from difficulties, toughness. Why would I say that resilience is a key factor in being a business owner? You must learn how to recover from difficulties. You must have tough skin when you are a business owner. You have to learn to deal with difficult customers, rude customers, even lazy employees sometimes. It comes with the job title, but it does not mean you have to embrace it. If you hire lazy employees, you can replace them with employees who take pride in your company and are not just there to collect an easy paycheck. We will talk about this a little later. Resilience is what helps you move on when you have had a tough day, you have to learn to shake the bad days off and give it another shot. You cannot, *must not* hold grudges or hang on to anger. Yes, you are entitled to get upset, but go to the bathroom; punch the air, scream, kick at the air, wash your face with some cold water, and get back out there and try again. Sometimes when I am being overwhelmed at work, I like to have a Coke and a smile. Literally, I will grab an ice-cold Coca-Cola and two Motrin and try again. Remember, it is not always going to be peaches and cream when you are the GO-TO person in the business. Not only will you have customers emailing you, sending you messages on Facebook messenger, text messaging you, and calling your business phone none stop; you will also have employees who need your immediate attention about something all the time, so if you do not deal with stress well, I suggest you invest in some lavender or lemon grass essential oil and a diffuser and learn how to woo-sa!

  Determination: firmness of purpose; resoluteness or the process of establishing something exactly by calculation or research. I would like to refer to the second definition: the process of establishing something exactly by calculation or research, except, I will be taking the "exactly" part out of my version of the definition. When you plan to start your business, whether it be an online bakery, online boutique, or an actual store front; you would have done all of this by research and calculating exactly how much you would invest into this business. That, my friends, is determination. But I could go a little deeper with determination.

It was your determination that had you up late hours of the night, searching for the perfect name and logo for your business. It was determination that had you soo excited to tell all your family and friends about your business idea. It was determination that had you passing out business cards on our "Networking Day." It was determination that had you baking and passing out samples of your products to prospects. It was determination that on your grand opening you were there with the biggest smile, looking up to the clouds saying, "Yes, I finally did it!" You see, determination is what pushed you into your destiny. Determination pushed you to be greater, and I am soo proud and excited to be able to share that moment with you. I must say although I was tired as all get out for my grand opening; I was bursting with sprinkles for excitement because I had achieved a lifetime goal that I had ever since I was in middle school baking brownies for my younger brother Ej and my nephew Rashawn. Thanks to you guys, I am a proud business owner of Tippy Cakes Bakery LLC.

One of the biggest problems or complaints I hear from people is they feel they are not good enough, or their product are not good enough, to start a business. I look at them with an empathetic heart and then I ask them why they feel that way. Most of the time, their reply is, "I don't know." So that leaves the door open for me to go in "Beast Mode" on them.

First, if you do not have the confidence in your own product or business, why should I? Why should customers purchase your product, your brand? They should not, right? This is where you must step up and take pride in your business, your product, and your brand. When you talk about your business, your product, and your brand, stand up straight and tall, not slouched over, make sure your shoulders are straight and broad, look your potential customer straight in the eye with a smile on your face, and give them three quick but powerful reasons why your product is the product they should be purchasing.

Let me give you an example: "Hello, my name is Tiffany, and I am the owner of Tippy Cakes Bakery. We are famous for our Gourmet Cupcakes, Ooey Gooey Fudge Brownies, and delicious homemade candy." Pretty easy, right? Did my introduction make you want to purchase a product or at least make you want to visit my website to see what I have to offer? It does not have to be a long drawn-out explanation of your business. Keep it short, simple, and sweet but remember to have a smile on your face and speak with confidence. Think of it as your chance to pitch your business idea to the sharks on the show *Shark Tank*. You may even have to stand in front of the mirror and practice your pitch until you have it memorized. Close your eyes, and say your pitch and once again--don't forget to smile! Your business, your brand and your product are ENOUGH for you and the world.

Let's be honest, is McDonald's cheeseburger the best burger you have ever had? No, but customers buy them every single day, and especially for their kids, so do not second guess what you have to offer the world. Be like Nike and "JUST DO IT"! If you still need a little help or a boost after reading this book, shoot me an email and we will practice this on a one-on-one basis. It is my goal, my dream to see you succeed. Unfortunately, I cannot be everywhere in the world, but that's why God led you to this book and allowed you to start your awesome business. You have a gift, a treat, and you need to be sharing your gift with the world. I have learned in my life, the more you give, the more you will receive. Learn to be a blessing to others and watch how God will return the favor of blessings to you.

Chapter 11: Tippy's Chocolate Chip Cookies (Learning How to Self-Motivate)

For many of my family and friends, they would say that I am a Motivating Cheerleader. I am always motivating and encouraging someone to do something even if it seems impossible. There is one thing I know for sure; NOTHING is impossible if you trust and believe. Faith the size of a mustard seed is all that you need. Have you ever seen a mustard seed? It is very, very small. So, imagine if you had faith the size of a grape, you could move mountains!

My Aunt Marie's husband, Calvin, had been talking about writing a book ever since the first or second time I met him. Years had passed but every time I saw him, he was still talking about writing his book. Family laughed and thought that he was just talking to hear himself talk, and after a life changing experienced happened to him, where he actually had a massive stroke and was bleeding on his brain, when he came out of the hospital and recovered, he finally wrote his book *Confessions of a Father's Omission* by Rufus Calvin Henderson (It's on Amazon by the way)! I am extremely proud of him because although it took him years to write his book, he never gave up on his dream of becoming an author and writing his first book. He had his first book signing at my bakery in which I am proud to say he sold out of books at his first book signing. Now, that is some amazing news!

So, if you needed a push in starting your dream, this should be some motivation! Rufus, who had a stroke and was in the hospital for weeks who even had slight memory loss was able to manifest his dream of becoming an author and write a book. He is currently in the process of writing his second book! The moral of his story is that you have to start somewhere, you may not have all the pieces to your puzzle at the very beginning, but keep prepping, planning and believing in your business and in yourself, and those pieces will start to come together perfectly. I am not saying that you will not have roadblocks and stumbling blocks on the way to your destination, you have to keep pushing. You know the saying: "Nothing worth having comes easy." Keep pushing, YOU GOT THIS!

When becoming an entrepreneur, you have to learn how to self-motivate because there will be days when you won't feel like getting out of bed or won't feel like putting in long hours, but because you are the boss and worker in the beginning, you will have to push yourself. You will have to learn how to address customers, even the not so happy customers, and give them number one customer satisfaction, because we all know negative reviews will spread faster than positive ones, and once you have negative buzz about your business, it will be hard to turn the negative reviews into positive ones. The good news is because you are the boss of your business, you can set your own schedule. I would suggest waking up earlier to have time to meditate, walk/jog, and plan for the day ahead. I also like to arrive to work earlier than opening so that it gives me time to bake fresh cupcakes, brownies, and cookies. It also gives me a chance to work on orders and things on my calendar. When you prepare in advance, you are prepared for anything that comes your way. You will also want to work on your time management, purchase you a scheduler, and try to work according to your scheduler.

Time	To Do Project	Completed By
9:00 AM	Make Cupcake Batter	Myself
10:00 AM	Make Cupcake Batter/ Bake Sugar Cookies	Myself
11:00 AM	Open Store/Count Register Turn on Open Sign	Assistant
12:00 PM	Check emails & voicemail	Myself
1:00 PM	Prep Chicken Salad for cooler	Deli Leader
2:00 PM	Prep Pimento Cheese for cooler	Deli Leader
3:00 PM	Make Brownies for next day	Assistant or Myself

This is just an example of a schedule you can implement into your daily routine. Even if you run an online business, it would be helpful to schedule your day so that you will not spend time scrolling on social media or checking emails all day. Trust me, time can get away from you if you do not plan accordingly. Use your time wisely. When I am at the bakery and my assistant is working, I make the best of my time by letting her work the front counter, helping and assisting the customers while I make up the cupcake batters, icings, prep my deli items, and decorate cakes. I also take advantage of making store runs. It is a blessing to have help in the bakery because whenever I need to step out, I can feel confident that someone will always be in the bakery to assist and help the customers and answer the telephone. By the end of my working day, I would have everything prepped for the next day, the kitchen swept, mopped, and ready for the next day.

January 2022

Sunday	Monday	Tuesday	Wednesday	Thursday	Friday	Saturday
					1	2
3	4	5	6	7	8	9
10	11	12	13	14	15	16
17	18	19	20	21	22	23
24	25	26	27	28	29	30
31						

This is a Calendar to help you keep track of all your important information. I use my calendar to keep track of Doctor Appointments, Cake Tasting Schedules, Bill Payments and so on. You can purchase your own calendar or go to Microsoft Word and download your calendar. You can even use the calendar on Yahoo or Google. I also have a calendar printed on my freezer at the bakery so that I keep track of all my cake orders for the month.

Tippy's Chocolate Chip Cookie Recipe

2 large eggs

2 cups all-purpose flour

¼ cup brown sugar

½ cup granulated sugar

Pinch of salt

2 cups chocolate chip morsels

2 teaspoons Cookie Nip/ or vanilla extract/ or almond vanilla extract

2 ½ tablespoons butter, softened

2 tbsp coffee creamer

Mix sugars, pinch of salt & butter together, add eggs one at a time, add all-purpose flour, then chocolate chip morsels, and 2 tablespoons coffee creamer. Once mixture is complete, scoop with small ice cream scoop, roll into balls, lay on parchment paper, and freeze for 20 minutes before baking. You can substitute M&M's for the chocolate chip morsels. Once chilled, put parchment paper on cookie sheet and bake for 8-10 minutes at 350 degrees.

Chapter 12: Raspberry Drizzle (Prepping and Planning for the Opening of Your Bakery)

If you are still reading this book, that means I was able to hold your interest long enough, I'm not as boring as you thought, or you are actually serious about getting your business off the ground! Whatever, the reason may be, I am humbly grateful that you are still on this journey with me. If you have been jotting down your ideas and answering the questions, you should have a good bit of information to help you get started with opening or starting your business. Whether you start with an online bakery or an actual storefront bakery, you have the resources to help you get started. Let's look over our checklist to make sure we have not forgotten anything.

- Business Name
- Business Location/ Storefront or Online
- Business Website & Social Media Presence
- Registering for an EIN
- Registering for your Sales Tax ID
- Opening a Business Checking Account
- Obtaining a Business License with your city
- Applying for an LLC or Sole Proprietorship
- Securing Funding for your Business
- Advertising for your Business
- Scheduling a Networking Day
- Setting up Vendor Accounts

You, my friend, have a lot of work ahead of you, but remember, "faith of a mustard seed" is all that you will need. And if you ever get stuck on something or start to feel self-doubt, reach out to one of your accountability partners or send me an email at Tippycakesbakery@yahoo.com and I will help cheer you on until you are replying with: "Yes I am Enough, My Business Will Succeed!" I have faith in you, Love, because I was once where you are! I pray that this book has helped you in some shape or form. I hope that this book made you smile and call your girlfriend or homeboy and tell them all about it. I hope this book was good enough for you to recommend it to other Bosses in the making. I hope that I was able to give you enough information to help you succeed in this bakery life. Remember, we don't have to be perfect (I am far from it) but I do want you to learn how to love yourself a little bit more, take breaks and rest more, drink more water, exercise more, learn to forgive and heal. Yes, Love, let all that old, negative energy go. If someone did you wrong, write them a letter stating that you forgive them and burn it up, throw it away, or do whatever you choose to do with it. Life is all about healing and forgiving and learning to love repeatedly. Remember the power of love is more powerful than any magic power you could ever possess. When you are feeling down, reflect on some of the chapters and bake your favorite recipe. Or bake your own recipe, package, and make money off it. Remember, drama and negativity will not make you any money, so do not give them any attention. I am truly thankful and delighted that you took the time to purchase my book and read it. Now I am going to need you to get in that kitchen, turn your oven on, put on your favorite apron, pull out your favorite mixer, and BAKE YOUR BUTT OFF!!

Love, Peace, and Happy Baking!

Tippy Cakes

Some of my favorite scriptures!

(2 Timothy 1:7) For God hath not given us the spirit of fear; but of power, and of love, and of a sound mind.

(Proverbs 31:25) She is clothed with strength and dignity; she can laugh at the days to come.

(Luke 11:10) For everyone that asketh receiveth; and he that seeketh findeth; and to him that knocketh it shall be opened.

(Ephesians 3:20) Now unto him that is able to do exceedingly abundantly above all that we ask or think.

(Philippians 4:19) And my God shall supply all your need according to his riches in glory by Jesus Christ.

I Am Grateful For Journal

My Shopping List

For Booking Information & Speaking Engagements

Email: TippyCakesBakery@yahoo.com

Facebook.com/TippyCakesBakery

Instagram.com/TippyCakes

Made in the USA
Las Vegas, NV
28 September 2021